IN PURSUIT
OF THE TRUTH

"And ye shall know the truth,
and the truth shall make you free."
John 8:32

LARRY L. DERAAD

authorHOUSE®

AuthorHouse™ LLC
1663 Liberty Drive
Bloomington, IN 47403
www.authorhouse.com
Phone: 1-800-839-8640

Published by AuthorHouse 11/25/2013

ISBN: 978-1-4918-3570-8 (sc)
ISBN: 978-1-4918-3571-5 (e)

TABLE OF CONTENTS

Dedication Prayer

Holy Father, I praise your name and worship you in truth and in spirit. I thank thee for your grace, and the gift of eternal life through the shed blood of your Son, Jesus Christ.

And

Holy Father, I thank thee for the many truths taught to me through the working of the Holy Spirit, truths that have strengthened and sustained me over the years.

And

Holy Father, I pray for your blessings upon these writings in this book. Father it's my prayer that you will take these truths recorded in your word and teach them to others of your elect and to build up your Kingdom on earth.

Amen!

DEDICATION

I dedicate this writing to the cause of Christ,

With a special thank you to my wife Charlotte K.

And to my pastor and good friend Elder Mike

Leinhauser, for his proofreading.

KNOW THE TRUTH

John 4:23-24 *"But the hour cometh, and now is, when the true worshippers shall worship the Father in spirit and in truth: for the Father seeketh such to worship him. (24) God is a spirit: and they that worship him must worship him in spirit and in truth."*

John 14:6 *"Jesus saith unto him, I am the way, the truth, and the life: no man cometh unto the Father, but by me."*

John 17:17 *"Sanctify them through thy truth: thy word is truth."*

Luke 1:3-4 *"It seemed good to me also, having had perfect understanding of all things from the very first, to write unto thee in order, most excellent Theophilus, (4) That thou mightiest know the certainty of those things, wherein thou hast been instructed."*

Note from the Author

The following chapters are a collection of tracks and pamphlets on a variety of subjects. These are writings and thoughts of mine during the retirement years of my life.

I pray you will read this collection and compare it to God's word, and let God's word be your only and final rule of truth.

Larry L DeRaad

FOREWORD

This book will be a delight or an offense to those that have chosen to read it. The content is written to put forth the truths of Holy Scripture. In this day and age of artificial churches it is a blessing to know there are still those who know and love the truth, and uphold it; Pro. 22.28 "Remove not the ancient landmark, which thy fathers have set." I commend Bro. DeRaad for his unswerving dedication to Biblical truth.

There are many religionists that sit in pews listening to their pastors preach what they want to hear and not what they should be hearing. Having not the Spirit of God in them, (preacher or hearer) how can they discern between truth and error? They need to hear it or read it and then may the Lord open their hearts to understanding.

This book is written to present these truths that they need to hear. Proverbs 23:23 "Buy the truth, and sell *it* not; *also* wisdom, and instruction, and understanding." A gracious God has given us a Holy Bible to be searched out daily for the truths written in it, these are written for our benefit.

Sadly many think all they need to do is attend some religious group each Sunday and all is well. It will not be well without hearing and heeding the truth, John 8:32 "And ye shall know the truth, and the truth shall make you free." The Bereans searched the Holy Scriptures to check up on the Apostles, Acts 17:11 "These were more noble than those in Thessalonica, in that they received the word with all readiness of mind, and searched the scriptures daily, whether those things were so." The Lord expects each and every one of His servants to do likewise, and who is a servant? John 3:3 "Jesus answered and said unto him, Verily, verily, I say unto thee, Except a man be born again, he cannot see (to know, i.e. get knowledge of, understand, perceive) the kingdom of God." Luke 24:45 "Then opened he their understanding, that they might understand the scriptures,"

Isaiah 55:1-3 "(1) Ho, every one that thirsteth, come ye to the waters, and he that hath no money; come ye, buy, and eat; yea, come, buy wine and milk without money and without price. (2) Wherefore do ye spend money for *that which is* not bread? And your labour for *that which* satisfieth not? Hearken diligently unto me, and eat ye *that which is* good, and let your soul delight itself in fatness, (3) Incline your ear, and come unto me: hear, and your soul shall live; and I will make an everlasting covenant with you, even the sure mercies of David." For those that have a desire to know Scriptural truth this book will open up some of them for you. Matthew 24:4 "And Jesus answered and said unto them, Take heed that no man deceive you,"

Mike Leinhauser

PREFACE

We are admonished in Holy writ to count the cost of discipleship. Luke 14:27-30, *"And whosoever doth not bear his cross, and come after me, cannot be my disciple. (28) For which of you, intending to build a tower, sitteth not down first, and counteth the cost, whether he have sufficient to finish it? (29) Lest haply, after he hath laid the foundation, and is not able to finish it, all that behold it begin to mock him, (30) Saying, This man began to build, and was not able to finish."* Jesus is instructing his disciples that they have a cross to bear, and a burden to share. The cross of discipleship will be heavy, and many times lonely. The price will cost us friends, neighbors, and even special loved ones.

Early on in my Christian walk I determined to pay whatever the cost may be. Although the price turned out to be greater than I originally imagined. I expected to lose friends, and I did. I expected to be looked down on, and I was. I expected others to bear false witness against me and they did. I was ready for this. What I didn't expect was my brothers and sisters in Christ to stand against me. That was the heaviest cross for me to bear. Other saints of God had predetermined for me that I should be ready to compromise. Walk down the center of the road. Don't make waves. Stand for truths, but sugar coat them first. Don't be controversial; meet the world halfway, etc., etc. I also determined not to do this. This world is full enough of soothsayers. The blessed truth is to be proclaimed at all costs. Compromising is not God's way. Truth in its entirety must be promulgated. I must speak out and publish this truth, whatever the cost.

This is the reason for this publication. To speak out, and defend the truths contained in God's word without compromise. After all I am the servant of God and him alone. I don't serve two masters. I love the hymn, "This world is not my home, and I'm just a passing through. My treasures are laid up somewhere beyond the blue."

Read John's account of John 15:18-20, *"If the world hate you, ye know that it hated me before it hated you. (19) If ye were of the world, the world would love his own: but because ye are not of the world, but I have chosen you out of the world, therefore the world hateth you."(20) Remember the word that I said unto you, The servant is not greater than his lord. If they have persecuted me, they will also persecute you; if they have kept my saying, they will keep yours also."*

If the world hated Christ, and it does, it will also hate me. If Jesus was persecuted, who am I that I shouldn't be?

The truths I write about are those so commonly mistaken, misunderstood, and ignored. Yet these are blessed truths that need to be rightly divided, and interrupted. These would not be controversial subjects if only we would be willing to believe God's word. CONTROVERSY ONLY EXISTS IN THE MINDS OF THOSE WHO WILL NOT SURRENDER THEIR OWN WILL, AND RECEIVE GOD'S.

I ask only that you compare with scripture what I'm about to say, and like the Bereans in Acts 17:11, *"Search the scriptures daily, whether those things were so."*

Clara H. Scott, says it best in her hymn, "Open My Eyes, That I May See"

Open my eyes, that I may see Glimpses of truth thou hast for me;
Place in my hand the wonderful key That shall unclasp, and set me free.
Silently now I wait for thee, Ready my God, Thy will to see;
Open my eyes, illumine me, Spirit divine!

Open my ears, that I may hear Voices of truth Thou sendest clear;
And while the wave-notes fall on my ear, Everything false will disappear.
Silently now I wait for thee, Ready my God, Thy will to see;
Open my ears, illumine me, Spirit divine!

Open my mouth, and let me bear Gladly the warm truth everywhere;
Open my heart, and let me prepare Love with thy children thus to share.
Silently now I wait for thee, Ready my God, Thy will to see;
Open my heart, illumine me, Spirit divine!

Chapter 1

My Life in Christ

An Autobiography

The DeRaad's (of which I am a part) were farmers up in Minnesota. We maintained around twenty two milk cows, two hundred hogs, some three hundred chickens all on two hundred and thirty-two acres of good cropland. Mom and Pop DeRaad had five children, two older girls Esther, and Beth, three sons, Virgil, Marvin, and me. My name is Larry. I'm the youngest, and considered as the baby of the family. Now, that usually means the most spoiled and the most favored of the family. However, I think this case is an exception to that rule.

My parents [especially my dad] made no bones about the fact that I was his greatest mistake. I shall never forget if I live to be a hundred years old my dad saying to me as he was milking the cows "If it weren't for you I wouldn't have to pull these teats." It's a fact that dad had a vasectomy sometime after Marvin was born, but between his vasectomy and his becoming sterile, I popped into the picture. Mom and Pop may not have planned for my existence, but God did. You can probably imagine how thankful I am, that abortion then wasn't an option. Although my parents were responsible for their actions and seen to my every physical need. They raised me as their own at least financially.

My eldest sister Esther also had a very hard place in our family. It turns out that she is my half-sister, and not of my dad's ancestry. She too had to deal with my dad's criticism. I guess that will forever put a special bond between her and me.

Then there are a sister and brother, Beth, and Virgil. They are a good sister and brother. They are quite older than I and as a result we were not all that close. Yet we had a love and admiration for one another as we should. I shall never forget Virgil teaching me to shoot a shot gun and a rifle. I enjoyed and appreciated that. My dad just never had time for such nonsense, and plainly didn't care.

My main problem however was with my next older brother Marvin. Marvin's physical stature was like that of my dad. Very stout and muscular was he. My opinion is that like my dad his body produced an extra portion of natural hormones and steroids which produced those muscles. I took after my mother in many of my bodily characteristics. Even in my being obese. At any rate Marvin was older and much stronger than I. He was given a nickname of "Meany" because he liked to beat on me just for the fun of it. His favorite place to hit me was on my shoulders. At least once every day or sometimes more I would feel the blunt of his fist on my shoulder. To him it was fun, but to me it meant throbbing pain. My parents at times would counsel with him to try and stop him, but it was to no avail. Although both mom and pop agreed that it was physiologically healthy for Marvin to have a ready place to vent his frustrations. I recall my dad commenting to others concerning the same. To him it may have been a joke, but to me it wasn't funny.

Marvin could do no wrong, and I could do no good. Soon I stopped trying. In fact I began to retaliate. I despised both my dad and Marvin. Again, recalling a comment from my dad about me. He said "Larry will always do the opposite of what you tell him to do." I thought yeah, but there's a good reason for that.

My parents liked to visit with friends and relatives, and brag up Marvin. They claimed "Marvin doesn't even need to read a book. All he needs to do is look at the pictures to find out what is in the book. But Larry isn't smart like Marvin. He will always find it hard. He's not smart like his brother." I hated him for that, and hated to go visit anyone for that very reason. What kind of parent would say such things within earshot of their children?

I soon learned my role in life. I believed what I was told. I was stupid by birth and I had to face up to that fact. Therefore Marvin must remain in the leadership role. When Marvin failed I must fail big time. When Marvin got into trouble I must get deeper into trouble. That was my course in life. As a freshman in high school Marvin failed his algebra class, so I must fail as well. Six weeks into my turn in Algebra I was dropped from the class. I never turned in a single assignment, and was very disruptive in class. I accomplished my task. I was playing my part. I fulfilled my parents' expectations for me. Also I must keep Marvin elevated above me or pay the price of Marvin's wrath. After all I didn't need the approval of man when I had God's approval. I had so completely abandon the idea of trying to impress anyone. I had only one agenda and that was to be pleasing to God. The bible says *"Love not the world, neither the things that are in the world. If any man love the world, the love of the Father is not in him."* I John 2:15, not loving this world came easy for me. I'm longing to be with Jesus. Again I share the sentiments of the Apostle Paul, *"For I am in a strait betwixt two, having a desire to depart, and to be with Christ; which is far better."*

My life took an abrupt turn for the better when I finally left home. God lead me to the love of my life, and she and I became one in marriage. She has been such a blessing and help mate to me. This last June, we celebrated our golden anniversary together.

After leaving Mom and Pop, I had to unlearn many lessons they taught me about myself and learn what my heavenly Father, through the working of the Holy Spirit, would teach me. I can't say enough about what Christ did in my life during this time. I will elaborate further on this a little later.

Over the years my shoulders grew weaker and more painful as time went by. Finally I had surgery on my right shoulder. The doctor said my shoulder was full of scar tissue, and the tendon that connected the bicep muscle to the shoulder was completely separated from the bone. Over the years the tendon had died and withered into a hunk of dead tissue. That was beyond help. Later, a second surgery on the right shoulder and then another on the left. I was told no other surgeries would ever help. I could have some cortisone shots to ease the pain from time to time, but that is all. The bicep muscle is supposed to do the work of lifting your arm above your shoulder. Because of the destroyed tendon the rotator cuff must compensate for the bicep muscle. The rotator muscle is a fraction of the bicep muscle, and it has permanent damage as well.

There were two other major obstacles in my life which had to be ever come. When at the age of about twelve years old, I lost my speech. I began to stutter, and stammer so badly that I couldn't communicate at all. It was right at the time of my life when I had taken up the tobacco habit, and everyone around me blamed it on the smoking habit. At first I thought, they were right, but I was hooked on nicotine. Then some time later, several years later, I think I found the real reason. It was also at that time of my life that I reached puberty, and the hormones were running wild in my body. This I think is the culprit. Whatever the reason, I was left speechless. This was a major problem for me in school. I had others snicker and laugh at me, and it was very embarrassing, and I got very bitter. I got into a lot of fights, and in much trouble as a result. I didn't hesitate in giving someone a knuckle breakfast at the first hint of a snicker.

However, as I grew older my speech slowly returned. My journey back was slow but sure. It took all of fifty years before I could speak without difficulty. God called me to preach the Gospel when I was around thirty years old, and was still having problems pronouncing many words without difficulty. I wondered how much of a problem this would be. I guess I felt like Moses when God sent him to deliver the Israelites from bondage in Egypt. Moses also had a speech impediment to overcome. God sent Aaron, Moses, brother to speak for him. God had to and did overcome my stuttering, and it never became a major problem for me to preach the truth of God's word. It only caused me to love God all the more.

One other major problem I had to ask God to help me with and to overcome was massive and severe headaches. It was July 21st of 1959 that five other friends of mine and I went swimming in a local swimming hole three o'clock in the morning. I was driving my dad's car and another friend was driving his dad's brand new 59 Ford. After swimming we headed for home. On the way we had a little race. He was leading the way and my car topped out at one hundred miles an hour. We all had the pedal to metal. Well, swimming always had a very calming, and relaxing effect on me. It seems I dozed off for a moment or so while driving, and right before coming to a "T" intersection. [Dead end] We came to a crashing stop real quick on the bank of the opposite side of the ditch. The other three friends in my car all survived and escaped death or serious injuries. All their injuries healed over the next few weeks or so. I learned later that I had one injury that would plague my life for many years, even the rest of my life. The very top vertebrae in my neck had been splintered. This would aggravate the muscles in my neck setting off tremendous tension headaches. The doctors said the location in my neck was inoperable without paralyzing me from the neck down. I had to learn to live with it. For the first three or four years it was a daily and unbearable fight, but gradually they became fewer in frequency, and even less severe. After six or seven years it was only two or three times a week, and usually less severe. By the time I reached forty years of age I had only two or three a month. By sixty I had completely gotten rid of the severe ones. What I have yet today are minor headaches, but yet aggravating ones. Usually two Tylenols will do the trick. However when they come they will stay for a few days. What I am left with today is severe arthritis that will plague me the rest of my life.

Needless to say, I'm looking forward to a new glorified body where no aches and pains will exist. I think I will even then be able to keep and hold a tune which now I can't. Should anyone not believe the truthfulness of Galatians 6:7-8, send them to me; I think I can clue them in on its truthfulness.

Galatians 6:7&8, says, *"Be not deceived; God is not mocked; for whatsoever a man soweth, that shall he also reap. (8) For he that soweth to the flesh shall of the flesh reap corruption; but he that soweth to the spirit shall of the spirit reap life everlasting."*

That's not to say that my younger years were all terrible years. I had a Heavenly Father that loved me with an unconditional love. It was that love that sustained and kept me. He gave to me all I ever needed. Proverbs 18:24 says *"There is a friend that sticketh closer than a brother."*

His name is Jesus, and he is the Christ my Saviour, Lord and friend. It was in my younger years [around twelve or so years old] when Christ came to me and gave to me the gift of eternal life. There is etched in my memory moments of greatest joy that this world could never understand. It was the peace of God that passes all understanding. Philippians 4:7. Anyone that hasn't experienced this peace will never, or could ever know what I'm talking about. No words could ever describe this peace that is given by God and only to those chosen by him to receive it. Salvation is an umbrella word. Salvation or regeneration includes repentance, Godly sorrow, faith in Christ, the fear of God, conviction of sin, and the love of God. All of these are given as gifts from God, and given to only those chosen of God. Etched in my memory are moments of the greatest peace any man could ever know. These were moments where God was embracing me and assuring me of his protection over me. He was sustaining me, and keeping me. I must have felt like Adam did in the Garden of Eden before the fall when he and God communed in the cool of the day, or like Noah did when he walked with God. Noah found grace in the eyes of the Lord, and so did I. I must confess here, I am not a Christian because of anything I have ever done or ever will do. I'm a Christian solely because God made me a Christian. All the credit and all the glory is his and his alone.

Needless to say, these moments of communing with God were isolated and private moments. No-one else would not ever understand nor will they yet today. The readers of this article that are not children of God will think of me as a lunatic with a deranged mind. But the loss is theirs.

There was so much that I didn't then know or understand that I've since learned over the course of my life. I can now put many of the pieces of the puzzle together, and see how God is working in my life, and I glorify God for it. For most of my adult life I thought the Lord saved me during a revival in Tennessee. However it was in the later years while a Pastor at a church in Arizona that the Lord revealed the truth to me. Those old memories of those moments in my younger days revealed the truth of when God really saved me. I recalled the love of God I had, the Godly sorrow, the repentance, the seeking after God, the desire to serve him. That was regeneration. I then realized I've been a child of God since a young man. I just had no-one to teach and guide me until I got away from the ungodly people around me and surround me with other Christians. Christian fellowship is so vitally important. The downside of this new found information was the fact of my lifestyle during those teenage years. These are years that I'm very much ashamed of. These are years that God has forgiven me for. This brings new life and meaning to the grace of God. Grace means unmerited favor, and certainly I don't deserve Gods favor. I shall never stop learning of God's grace.

It was when I was twenty-five years old during an old time revival in Tennessee that I rededicated my life to Christ as best as I ever could. It was Jesus that said in Matthew 11:29 *"Take my yoke upon you, and LEARN OF ME; for I am meek and lowly in heart, and ye shall find rest for your souls."* So I determined to first learn of him, and never got over it. Then reading in II Timothy 2:15, I read *"Study to show thyself approved unto God, a workman that needeth not to be ashamed, rightly dividing the word of truth."* I sought only God's approval, and never again to be ashamed. Over the years I have failed in this quest but God never forsakes me. I keep trying, and God keeps blessing me. God's truth is everything to me and without truth there remains nothing. Then I read in Matthew 16:18 where Jesus said *"I will build my church and the gates of Hades will not prevail against it."* Immediately I realized the church Jesus built must still be here, but where is it? I must find it for there is no greater place for me to be than in his church. I must find it at all costs. Jesus promised her [his church] a perpetual existence so she must be here. My life's quest if need be is to locate and join her. I've uprooted and moved my family across America more than once in my search. I've been in and out of denominations, conventions, associations, Independent organizations and movements of all sorts. I had to be confident that I was a part of the church that Jesus built. Finally I came across a church and groups of churches that agreed with what the New Testament taught, and the good news didn't stop here. They had a linage that took them all the way back to the Apostles and to Christ himself. Man could start counterfeit churches but only Christ started his church. These churches followed the pattern of churches found in the New Testament. Only Christ is the head and founder of His church and his church only. I was confident my search was over. Then I read in Ephesians 3:21 *"Unto him be glory in the church throughout all ages, world without end.* AMEN." It is only know that I can glorify Christ in his church.

Over the years of my Christian service I've been both encouraged and discouraged. Encouragement comes from Jesus Christ as I serve him in his church. Discouragements come from what I see and hear around me from other so-called pastors and members of their counterfeit, protestant and catholic churches. Case in point, I had a conversation with a certain pastor concerning God's plan of salvation. We agreed that baptism, church membership, honesty, goodness or any such thing would never save anyone. I was mystified with his agreement. I asked him how he could justify his churches standing concerning this. He said that there were many things that he disagreed with concerning what his church believed and taught but that he was obligated to the church leaders to teach what they demanded. This is what I mean by discouragement. He just took Christ from being the head of the church and applied it to mere man. His denomination does not include the church Jesus built. Now, I'm sure he's not an isolated case. Anyone who surrounds himself with the scriptures must sooner or later understand enough to be uncomfortable in their counterfeit man made churches. It's not enough that they are lying to their congregations, but think of the ones being lied to. Truth has no hold on them. These are soothsayers. To them it's a numbers game. The more members in their congregations the more successful they appear, and they know how to appeal to the flesh. It's "If it feels good do it," mentality that brings the heathen in by the droves. New Testament churches were to consist of saved, born again, regenerated, members only. Christian's who have been scripturally immersed in water [baptized] after conversion are the only fit subjects to be members of the Church that Jesus built. That's the New Testament pattern of the Church that Jesus built. This alone excludes all Catholic, and protestant churches. It is after this that you gain an unquenchable thirst to know more of Christ and his church. How a Christian could possible ever say," I don't care to know more about the Saviour, or about God." is more than I can understand. What's lacking is the fear of God, and the love of God. They are still in their sins, and under the wrath of God.

During my retirement years I've been writing some religious tracks and pamphlets concerning what others would call very controversial subjects. First it's interesting to note that nothing is controversial if you're willing to take scriptures word for it. It's only when we don't want to believe God or his word that it becomes controversial. I write about what nobody else wants you to know. I'm not doing this for notoriety or the praise of men. In fact it will cause men to hate me. It's God's truth that motivates me simply because God wants it that way.

Philippians 2:13 *"For it is God that worketh in you both to will, and to do of his good pleasure."*

Therefore all glory goes to God.

I have since, but only by the grace of God, forgiven my parents and my brother. I hold no animosity or hostility toward them. I Timothy 1:14, expresses it this way *"And the grace of our Lord was exceeding abundant with faith and love which is in Christ Jesus"* Forgiveness didn't come easy. It was only after much prayer and soul searching that I was able to turn away from it.

This writing isn't to denigrate my parents or my brother, but to show Christ in my life. Matthew 7:47, Describes a woman deep in sin and received forgiveness for those sins. Jesus said she loves much because she was forgiven much. She washed the feet of Jesus with her tears, and dried his feet with the hairs of her head. It's amazing what the love of Christ will cause us to do. My sins which were and are many have been forgiven me, and as a result Christ is everything to me. I love Him more than anything of this world, even life itself.

This is a true story with a happy ending. On second thought, it's a true story without an ending. What Jesus gave to me is life eternal, life everlasting. Once been described as fourteen forever's, and that's a long time.

By this writing, I'm not, at least I don't think I am, feeling sorry for myself and crying in my milk. Maturity should cause one to stop blaming others for his own mistakes and failures. Certainly I rank high in sins and mistakes in my life. I share the sentiments of the Apostle Paul in saying I am the chief of sinners. I Corinthians 15:9 and I Timothy 1:15. Many times I have counseled others to forgive themselves when God has forgiven them. This very well may be the hardest thing for me to do. I deeply deplore the sins of my past life, and find it very hard to forgive myself. Even though I know God has forgiven me.

I have left my former life behind, and even though it's hard to walk away from I have made every effort to do so. My present life is built around God's grace and mercy. Apostle Paul said it best *"By the grace of God, I am what I am."* I Corinthians 15:10

CHAPTER 2

No Private
Interpretation

II Peter 1:20-21 *"Knowing this first, that no prophecy of the scriptures is of any private interpretation. (21) For the prophecy came not in old time by the will of man: but holy men of God spake as they were moved by the Holy Ghost."*

Countless times I have encountered those who call themselves Christians and yet have no idea what truths are revealed in holy writ. There are multitudes of reasons for this condition. In the forefront of this long list of reasons is the lack of concern and caring. Its one thing to say you are a Christian and quite another to be one. These are professors but not possessors. Those who say they are Christians and are not are hypocrites, and under the wrath of God and awaiting their final doom. Their eyes are blinded, their ears are stopped, their hearts are hardened, and their minds are made dull. These have no idea of God or His word, and simply don't care. As long as they remain in this condition they are under the wrath of a just and angry God. This means they are completely dependent upon God's grace and mercy. Should God be pleased to leave them in their natural condition they are without hope of ever being redeemed.

I Corinthians 2:14 *"But the natural man receiveth not the things of the Spirit of God: for they are foolishness unto him: neither can he know them, because they are spiritually discerned."*

Another reason for their lack of knowledge is their slothfulness (laziness). This is closely akin to the lack of concern, caring, and ability with the natural unregenerate man. Slothfulness and a lack of caring go hand in hand, and are characteristics of a natural and lost man.

Also, the cares of this world will choke out both the time and effort needed in studying the word of God. They see no need of knowing God or his word. Couple this with the fact that they are blind, deaf, and dumb to all spiritual matters. They have no capability of ever knowing God's truth. Yet they are under the mistaken idea that they know more than God, and see no need of a Saviour.

It is completely understandable for us to expect no spiritual understanding on their part. So why is it even mentioned in this study of the true interpretation of God's word? I mention this because of the influence that the natural and lost people have on the newly saved and as yet babes in Christ. These are not immune to the influences of the lost. These are the blind leading the blind. Those who are knowledgeable and matured in God's word need to counsel with these new learners of scripture.

Read again our text. II Peter 1:20-21 *"Knowing this first, that no prophecy of scripture is of any private interpretation.(21) For the scripture came not in old time by the will of man: but holy men of God spake as they were moved by the Holy Ghost."*

I am very thankful to be an American. America has a constitution which guarantees us religious liberty. That is freedom to follow the dictates of our hearts. I completely agree with this and would freely give my life to defend it. But according to our text, God doesn't give us this same right. God obligates us and makes us responsible to know, believe, and obey His word. We have no God given right to believe whatever fits our fancy. When God judges this world He will judge according to His word, and not our fancies. Not what we would like the truth to be, but what really is true.

Proverbs 14:12 *"There is a way which seemeth right unto a man, but the end thereof are the ways of death."*

God may and as yet does allow man to follow every wind of doctrine when their own ideas run contrary to scripture. However in the fullness of time God will judge and condemn all those doctrines of the devil, and those who proclaim them.

Ephesians 4:14 *"That we henceforth be no more children, tossed to and fro, and carried about with every wind of doctrine, by the sleight of men, and cunning craftiness, whereby they lie in wait to deceive;"*

In every doctrine under heaven and taught in scripture, there exists but one true interpretation and this interpretation isn't left up to us. Scripture will interpret scripture. It is for this very reason the Apostle Paul instructed Timothy to study in-depth (not just casual reading) to show himself approved unto God.

> II Timothy 2:15-16 *"Study to shew thyself approved unto God, a workman that needeth not to be ashamed, rightly dividing the word of truth. (16) But shun profane and vain babblings: for they will increase unto more ungodliness."*

Search out the truth and shun profane and vain babblings. Untruths will always lead to ungodliness. One lie will always lead to another lie.

> Proverbs 23:23 *"Buy the truth, and sell it not, also wisdom, and instruction, and understanding."*

The very reason for this short chapter is to encourage you to study and search out the truth from God's word. The Bible is the only place to find God's truth. The Bible will interpret itself if studied correctly. We must learn the mind of Christ on any given doctrine.

> Philippians 2:5 *"Let this mind be in you, which was also in Christ Jesus:"*

To accomplish this we need to carefully examine every verse in the Bible which pertains to any given subject. Only then we can know the mind of Christ on this subject.

Don't look from within yourself, or your fleshly desires, or from your heart, or from your own understanding, or from your likes or dislikes. Even your preconceived ideas will lead you astray. The Holy Spirit alone will lead us unto all truths, and those truths are revealed in God's word.

The Bereans searched the scriptures daily, whether those things were so.

Acts 17:11 *"These were more noble than those in Thessalonica, in that they received the word with all readiness of mind, and searched the scriptures daily, whether those things were so."*

Your level of Biblical knowledge is very much limited to your level of "want to", or your level of desire to know God's truth. It's so sad, but so true; most of God's saints will search out God's word until they become satisfied in their own minds whether or not they have reached the whole truth.

There is no truth in scripture that cannot be reached provided we want it badly enough to search, study, believe, serve, and obey God, and His word.

John 7:17 *"If any man will do his will, he shall know of the doctrine, whether it be of God, or whether I speak of myself."*

I implore you to compare what I'm about to say in the following chapters of this brief writing. Compare it with God's word, and let God's word be your only rule of faith, order, and practice. If God's word says it, that settles it.

CHAPTER 3

The God of the Bible

Daniel 4:35 *"And all the inhabitants of the earth are reputed as nothing; and He doeth according to his will in the army of heaven, and among the inhabitants of the earth; and none can stay his hand, or say unto him, What doest thou."*

Isaiah 14:27 *"For the Lord of host hath purposed, and who shall disannul it? And his hand is stretched out, and who shall turn it back?"*

Isaiah 40:22 *"It is he that sitteth upon the circle of the earth, and the inhabitants thereof are as grasshoppers; that stretcheth out the heavens as a curtain, and spreadeth them out as a tent to dwell in;"*

Isaiah 46:10-11 *"Declaring the end from the beginning, and from ancient times the things that are not yet done, saying, My counsel shall stand, and I will do all my pleasure: (11) Calling a ravenous bird from the east, the man that executeth my counsel from a far country: yea, I have spoken it, I will also bring it to pass: I have purposed it, I will also do it".*

T he God of the Bible is altogether different from the god that the natural man perceives him to be. The natural unregenerate man knows little, or nothing of the true God of all creation.

I Corinthian 2:14 *"But the natural man receiveth not the things of the spirit of God, for they are foolishness unto him, neither can he know them; because they are spiritually discerned."*

The natural man in his depraved state can only imagine what his god is. He sees his god through sinful eyes. He supposes in his mind what he wants his god to be, and to him that's what he is. He is not capable of knowing the true God of the bible. His god is a figment of his own imagination. He may even learn to love his idea of his god. However his nature compels him to be at odds with and in a state of enmity against the God of the Bible.

Roman 8:7 *"Because the carnal mind is enmity (enemy) against God, for it is not subject to the law of God, neither indeed can it be."* (Emphasis mine L.D.)

The natural man sees God through sinful and blinded eyes, blinded by Satan.

II Corinthian 4:3-4 *"But if the gospel be hid, it is hid to them that are lost: (4) In whom the god of this world hath blinded the minds of them which believe not, lest the light of the glorious gospel of Christ, who is the image of God, should shine unto them."*

So the lost can only imagine in his own sinful mind what his god truly is. He therefore makes his god into an image of his own self.

Psalm 50:21b *"Thou thoughtest that I was altogether such an one as thyself;"*

He summarizes, surely God has seen all my good points, and understands my situations, and by mercy forgives all my sins. After all, my good points far outweigh the other offences.

However, little is known of God's Holiness, righteousness and justice. If a holy God were to overlook, or excuse sin simply through mercy, He could not be a righteous; or just God. For God to be a holy, righteous, and just God, He must punish sin with death.

Roman 6:23 *"For the wages of sin is death, but the gift of God is eternal life through Jesus Christ our Lord."*

The God of the bible believes in and exercises the death penalty for all sinners. God is absolute perfection, and will accept nothing but absolute perfection from his creation. Adam was created in holiness, but fell from that holy estate, and became a sinful being. He received a sinful nature, and if left to himself could or would never be able to reunite with God. So, what was God to do? Must He now accept less from his creation? Yet, God changes not. So, we must conclude, if one little evil thought were to enter your mind anytime during your lifetime, and that was still to your charge at end of life's pathway, heaven could never be your home. God will never allow sin in his kingdom. All the good you thought you did in your life would mean nothing. God must remain true to his holiness, righteousness and justice or cease to be God.

Another attribute of God is his wrath. His wrath is against any and all ungodliness or unrighteousness of men.

Roman 1:18 *"For the wrath of God is revealed from heaven against all ungodliness and unrighteousness of men, who hold the truth in unrighteousness;"*

God's mercy and forgiveness in no way removes the sentence of death for sin. The wages of sin is still death. Here lies the reason Christ had to come and die. His death and shed blood paid for my sins. My sins were paid by his death on the cross, and I am forgiven, and set free. It was God's grace that sent Christ to the cross so His mercy could forgive my sins without offending His holiness, righteousness, or justice. His wrath was redirected from me to Christ while on the cross. Thus all of Gods attributes were fully satisfied. Here is the plan of salvation God has purposed for His elect.

Understanding now His sovereignty; who is included in His plan of salvation? It is supposed that the human race is all included, but not so. Only those believing in Christ have eternal life.

John 3:16 *"For God so loved the world, that he gave his only begotten Son, that* WHOSOEVER BELIEVETH *in Him should not perish, but have everlasting life."* (Emphasis mine L.D.)

Ephesians 2:8 *"For by grace are ye saved through faith."*

Those nonbelievers and those without faith stand already condemned, and are awaiting God's wrath.

John 3:36 *"He that believeth on the Son hath everlasting life: and he that believeth not the Son shall not see life: but the* WRATH OF GOD ABIDETH ON HIM." (Emphasis mine L.D.)

John 3:18 *"He that believeth on Him is not condemned: but he that believeth not is* CONDEMNED ALREADY, *because he hath not believed in the name of the only begotten Son of God."* (Emphasis mine L.D.)

Hebrews 10:31 *"It is a fearful thing to fall into the hands of the living God."*

Only those believing in Christ (not just acknowledging) have everlasting life. Understand that faith is not something you can do of your own accord.

Eternal life and everything necessary to obtain it are gifts given of the Father, and these gifts are not given across the board to everyone. God is a sovereign God and does as He pleases to whomever He pleases, and whenever He pleases. Some are made vessels unto honor and some vessels unto dishonor as it pleases Him.

Romans 9:21 *"Hath not the potter power over the clay, of the same lump to make one vessel unto honour, and another unto dishonour."*

Romans 9:18 *"Therefore hath He mercy on whom He will have mercy, and whom He will He hardeneth."*

Before the creation of the universe God chose a certain innumerable multitude unto salvation through Jesus Christ our Lord. All the rest He left to their sinful nature and to their just condemnation. A question needs to be asked, why did Jesus come and die on the cross? What was His purpose? Most people will say to rescue the human race from death and condemnation. If so, Christ has failed. Most of the human race is under the wrath of a just God.

Matthew 7:13-14 *"Enter ye in at the strait gate: for wide is the gate, and broad is the way, that leadeth to destruction, and* MANY THERE BE WHICH GO IN THEREAT: *Because strait is the gate, and narrow is the way, which leadeth unto life,* AND FEW THERE BE THAT FIND IT." (Emphasis mine L.D.)

A small percent of the human race God chose to redeem by sending Christ to die in their behalf, as their substitute, on the cross. Therefore the penalty of death for my sins was paid for by Christ. I am one of those that the Holy Spirit brought to the Father through Jesus the Son. This makes my salvation WHOLLY of God.

Ephesians 2:8-9 *"For by grace are ye saved through faith, and that not of yourselves: It is the gift of God. (9) Not of works, lest any man should boast."*

There is nothing within myself that makes me worthy of the master's love.

Ephesians 1:4-5 *"According as He hath chosen us (me) in Him before the foundation of the world, that we should be holy and without blame before him in love. (5) Having* PREDISTINATED *us unto the adoption of children by Jesus Christ to himself,* ACCORDING TO THE GOOD PLEASURE OF HIS WILL" (Emphasis mine L.D.)

II Timothy 1:9 *"Who hath saved us, and called us with an holy calling, not according to our works, but according to his own purpose and grace, which was given us in Christ Jesus before the world began,"*

Titus 3:5 *"Not by works of righteousness which we have done, but according to his mercy he saved us, by the washing of regeneration, and renewing of the Holy Ghost;"*

To know why, or who God chose, to bring to Christ is to get into the mind of God. It is enough for us to know that God is a sovereign God and has the right to do as he pleases without asking for our approval or permission. He is the potter and we are the clay. Does this offend you? Many are offended at the thought of a sovereign God. God is not obligated to anyone for anything. God would be completely gracious, merciful, holy, and just to have condemned the entire human race, and saved no one.

Daniel 4:35 *"And all the inhabitants of the earth are reputed as nothing; and he doeth according to his will in the army of heaven, and among the inhabitants of the earth; and none can stay his hand, or say unto him, what doest thou?"*

It's assumed that God just cannot help but love us. That's a pleasant thought, but it's not true. John 3:16 is the most quoted verse in all the bible, and also the most misunderstood verse. What does *"God so loved the world"* mean? First get the context right. Jesus was speaking to Nicodemus, a ruler of the Jews. The Jews held to the Old Testament belief that salvation is of the Jews. Anything outside of the borders of Israel was considered as the world. Jesus was correcting the notion that Gods love ended at the boarders of Israel. God's love was worldwide in scope, every nation, every tongue; every nationality of people has those who God loves. To say this includes every person is to add something to scripture that is not there.

Romans 3:29 *"Is he the God of the Jews only? Is he not also of the Gentiles? Yes, of the Gentiles also:"*

Acts 10:34-35 *"Then Peter opened his mouth, and said, Of truth I perceive that God is no respecter of persons: (35) But in every nation he that feareth him, and worketh righteousness, is accepted with him."*

God's love doesn't stop at the boarders of Israel nor does it exclude any nation. That's not to say God loves every person.

Romans 9:13 *"As it is written, Jacob have I loved, but Esau have I hated."*

Hated means to detest and despise. God loves those of his own choosing and according to his own good pleasure without anything seen, or foreseen within them.

Psalms 5:5b *"thou hatest all workers of iniquity."*

Psalms 7:11 *"God judgeth the righteous, and God is angry with the wicked every day."*

Revelation 3:19 *"AS MANY AS I LOVE, I rebuke and chasten:"* (Emphasis mine L.D.)

God chastens all He loves, but doesn't chasten everyone.

Hebrews 12:6-8 *"For whom the Lord loveth He chasteneth, and scourgeth every son whom He receiveth. If ye endure chastening, God dealeth with you as with sons; for what son is he whom the Father chasteneth not? But if ye be without chastisement, whereof all are partakers, then are ye bastards, and not sons."*

Now do you still love the God of the bible? Is he the God of your life? Or is He a different God than you imagined?

Before this world began, God thought of me. He considered me, and put His love upon me. Then in the fullness of time He put in me a heart of flesh that would love Him. He gave me Godly sorrow over my sins. He gave me faith in His dear Son. He granted to me true repentance. He quickened my soul, and gave me spiritual and eternal life. Then he gave me a desire to do of His good pleasure.

Philippians 2:13 *"For it is God which worketh in you both to will and to do of his good pleasure."*

CHAPTER 4

Immutability of God

Pertaining to Redemption

F ew if anyone fully understands God's complete plan to redeem the lost from his deserved condemnation. Mortal man views God from his own perspective, and sees only what would benefit him. Couple this with the fact that his eyes are blinded by the god of this world (Satan)

> John 12:40 *"He hath blinded their eyes, and hardened their heart; that they should not see with their eyes, nor understand with their heart, and be converted and I should heal them"*

> II Corinthians 4:4 *"In whom the god of this world hath blinded the minds of them which believe not, lest the light of the glorious gospel of Christ, who is the image of God, should shine unto them."*

Man imagines a God with good intensions that created a good universe, but when man came along and changed all that. God had to scrape plan 'A' and resort to plan 'B' Little do they know, plan 'A' is still in effect and working perfectly.

In this short script I hope to show that man doesn't change God, God changes men.

> Psalm 33:11 *"The counsel of the Lord standeth forever, the thoughts of His heart to all generations."*

> Psalm 102:27 *"But thou art the same, thy years shall have no end."*

> Malachi 3:6 *"For I am the Lord, I change not; therefore ye sons of Jacob are not consumed."*

> Hebrews 1:12 *"And as a vesture shalt thou hold them up, and they shall be changed: but thou art the same, and thy years shall not fail."*

Hebrews 13:8 *"Jesus Christ the same yesterday, and today, and forever."*

James 1:17 *"Every good gift, and every perfect gift is from above, and cometh down from the Father of lights, with whom is no variableness, neither shadow of turning."*

God is the same yesterday, today, and forever. The scriptures are not silent concerning this fact, and we need to take heed of this. No greater mistake could be made than to think God can be manipulated by good intensions or otherwise.

Daniel 4:35 *"And all the inhabitants of the earth are reputed as nothing: and he doeth according to His will in the army of heaven, and among the inhabitants of the earth: and none can stay his hand, or say unto him, What doest thou?"*

God is both immutable and sovereign

God does exactly as He chooses, When He chooses, wherever He chooses, and to whomever He chooses, and doesn't need our approval, or permission. God is not pressured by popular demand nor public opinion.

Psalm 115:3 *"But our God is in the heavens: He hath done whatsoever He hath pleased."*

Psalm135:6 *"Whatsoever the Lord pleased, that did He in heaven, and in the earth, in the seas, and all deep places."*

Isaiah 46:10-11, *"Declaring the end from the beginning, and from ancient times the things that are not yet done, saying, My counsel shall stand, and I will do all my pleasure: (11) Calling a ravenous bird from the east, the man that executeth my counsel from a far country: yea, I have spoken it, I will also bring it to pass; I have purposed it, I will also do it."*

God is a complete God

God cannot be added to, nor taken from. God never improves over time. Is never caught off guard or surprised, and nothing ever occurs to God.

God is Omni science [knows all things]. Omni present [all over in all places at the same time.], and Omni potent [all powerful and almighty] God is ever existent and self-existent. There is nothing outside of God that wasn't created by God. He is the supreme God with no limitations of power or authority.

God is a trinity

There are three persons yet one God within the three: God the Father, God the Son, and God the Holy Ghost; yet one God. Each one is God and all three are God. All three are equal in power and might and all three are in agreement.

> Genesis1:26 *"And God said, let us make man in our image after our likeness: and let them have dominion over the fish of the sea, and over the fowl of the air, and over the cattle, and over all the earth, and over every creeping thing that creepeth upon the earth."*

The Godhead is present and active. The "US' and 'OUR' reveal the trinity of the Godhead. God the Father is speaking to God the Son and the God the Holy Ghost saying *"let us make man in our image."* Let us make man a trinity. That is three in one (Body, soul and spirit) yet one being.

God created in Holiness

All of God's creation was created holy and perfect. As you read the creation account in Genisis1:1-31. You should notice five times God referred to His creation as being good. In verses 10; 12; 18; 21, and 25; God created Adam and then Eve and put them in a perfect environment *"and behold it was very good."* Genesis 1:25

Now the all-important question, if God created all things in Holiness, SHOULDN'T GOD HAVE THE RIGHT TO EXPECT HOLINESS IN RETURN? Most men would say yes, but that was before sin entered into the world. Once sin appeared man changed so God had to adapt Himself to that change. It became impossible for man to be perfect so God had to adapt His expectations to man's capabilities. Sounds good except for one thing, God doesn't change and never will change at any cost. NEVER, EVER.

The fall of man

By rebelling against God, Adam and Eve fell from that holy estate that God had created them in and received a nature that was completely anti-God and anti-responsive to God. God had told them not to eat of the tree of the knowledge of good and evil for the day they eat of it they would surely die. That same day they died a spiritual death. No longer in the image of God, but now they are only two fold rather than a trinity. They are spiritually dead. Man's nature was also changed to that of being opposed to God.

> I Corinthians 2:14 *"But the natural man receiveth not the things of the spirit of God; for they are foolishness unto him: neither can he know them, because they spiritually discerned."*

> Romans 8:7 *"Because the carnal mind is enmity against God: for it is not subject to the law of God, neither indeed can be."*

As a result of the fall man has become a slave to his sinful nature and cannot escape from it. Only through faith in Jesus Christ, can we obtain Christian liberty.

> Romans 8:21 *"Because the creature itself also shall be delivered from the bondage of corruption unto the glorious liberty of the children of God."*

God set in place the penalty for sin before the fall. Genesis 2:17 *"For in the day that thou eatest thereof thou salt surely die."* It's still true today. Romans 3:23, *"For the wages of sin is death."* God doesn't change and neither does the penalty for sin.

The result of sin in the world is death, pain, suffering, sorrow, and shame. So, what's the answer? What's God to do? Man's only hope of redemption is for God to return him back to a state of holiness where God could receive him. This can only be accomplished by the death of His Son Jesus Christ on the cross, and then only after Christ fulfilled the whole law perfectly and without sin, and then to bear our sin on the cross to pay the ultimate price of His shed blood on the cross in our behalf.

Hebrews 9:22, *"And almost all things are by the law purged with blood; and without shedding of blood is no remission."*

The Attributes of God

We need to have an understanding of the attributes of God. These are many more than we will name hear, but we will list some of them. Some of God's attributes included His love [God is love], grace, mercy, forgiveness, kindness, compassion, long suffering, gentle, and patience, etc. Still others include His wrath, anger, vengeance, justice, and righteousness. There seems to be two lists of attributes. One list that men love and one man would rather not consider. Yet it is all the same God.

God is also a God of harmony. All of God's attributes are always in complete agreement. Not one of them is opposed to the others. God's love and His wrath complement each other. God is a God of forgiveness and a God of anger, justice and vengeance. We like to think of His love, grace, and mercy, but shudder at His wrath and justice.

Suppose you were sitting in a courtroom witnessing a murder trial. The defendant was accused of murder in the first degree. The evidence included a murder weapon with his fingerprints on it. Three eye-witnesses testified. The motive was explained, and the forensic evidence shown. After a short time of deliberation the jurors reached a guilty verdict. The judge proclaimed him guilty as charged, but set him free saying we are to be a forgiving people. The judge can be loving, forgiving, full of mercy kind, and compassionate, but not just. To be just he would have to punish the crime. The same is true with God and our sins. Never has there ever been a sin, or ever will be a sin that doesn't pay the price of death *"For the wages of sin is death."* To not punish sin is to offend the justice of God. God's completeness and His harmony would have been destroyed. And God would be divided against himself. This begs the question, How can God be just and the justifier of man?

Romans 3:26 *"To declare, I say, at this time his righteousness: that he might be just, and the justifier of him which believeth in Jesus."*

There is a way God can be just and the justifier of him which believeth in Christ.

Jesus our Mediator

A mediator is a go between that brings two parties together. Man has been separated from God because of sin. Without a mediator man and God would be eternally separated without any hope of reconciliation.

I Timothy 2:5 *"For there is one God, and one mediator between God and man, the man Christ Jesus;"*

Jesus paid the ultimate price for my sin while on the cross. My sin debt has been paid. Jesus was my substitute. He made full payment for my sins. Jesus died that I might live and live eternally.

The good news doesn't stop there. Not only did Jesus take my sins to the cross, but He gave to me His righteousness. That is He has charged to my account His righteousness.

II Corinthians 5:21 *"For he hath made him to be sin for us, who knew no sin; that we might be made the righteousness of Christ in him."*

By the faith of Christ in me, God declares me righteous. Not that I am righteous within myself, but that God declares me righteous. Romans 3:26 *"To declare, I say, at this time, his righteousness; that he might be just, and the justifier of him which believeth in Jesus."* It's a declaration of God because of what Jesus did on my behalf. We are made acceptable in Christ.

God has reversed the effect of the fall, and returned us to holiness again. Men didn't change God, God changed man. Situations or circumstances don't change God; God changes situations and circumstances to meet His purpose. When God looks at his redeemed, what does He see? Does He see their sins? No, Jesus paid their sins and took them from them. Then what does God see? He sees in them the righteousness of Christ. He sees when Christ made the blind to see, the deaf to hear, the lame to walk, the lepers to be healed, the dead raised to life, and the multitudes fed. By the faith of Christ, his elect would be made the righteousness of Christ.

God then remains just and the justifier of His elect, this is the working of the Triune God to redeem man. God the Father planned man's redemption, God the Son paid the price for man's redemption, and God the Holy Spirit brought about man's redemption.

We are truly saved because of the grace of God, and through the faith of Christ. This is God's plan of salvation.

Titus 3:5-7 *"Not by works of righteousness which we have done, but according to His mercy he saved us, by the washing of regeneration, and the renewing of the Holy Ghost; (6) Which he shed on us abundantly through Jesus Christ our Saviour; (7) That being justified by His grace, we should be made heirs according to the hope of eternal life."*

Romans 3:27 and 28 *"Where is boasting then? It is excluded. By what law? Of works? Nay: but the law of faith. (28) Therefore we conclude that a man is justified by faith without the deeds of the law."*

This removes all pride and self-boasting within ourselves. I am not a Christian because of anything I have ever done, or ever will do. Simply because He chose me before He created the world.

Ephesians 1:4-6 *"According as He hath chosen us in him before the foundation of the world, that we should be holy and without blame before him in love: (5) Having predestinated us unto the adoption of children by Jesus Christ to himself, according to the good pleasure of his will. (6) To the praise of the glory of his grace, wherein he hath made us accepted in the beloved."*

God called His people to be holy and without blame, and then brought it into reality. Thus salvation is wholly of God without any mixture of works from man. All this is according to the good pleasure of His will.

Conclusion

Man in his depraved nature and self-pride would like to receive his own glory, and credit himself for his salvation. Supposing Christ died for the entire human race and all man has to do is make the right chose and behold he's saved. This makes salvation of works rather than grace.

Did Christ die for everyone? If so everyone would be saved. Jesus would have paid the penalty for all sins and everyone's sin would be paid. In truth Jesus paid for the sins of those given to Him by the Father.

John 17:2b, 6, 9, 11, 12, 20 and 24

2b *". . . that He should give eternal life to as many as thou hast given him."*
6 *"Unto the men which thou gavest them me;"*

9 *"I pray for them: I pray not for the world, but for them which thou hast given me; for they are thine."*
11 *"Keep through thine own name those whom thou hast given me, that they may be one as we are."*
12 *"Those that thou gavest me I have kept, and none of them is lost."*
20 *"Neither I pray for these alone, but for them also which shall believe on me through their words."*
24 *"Father, I will that they also, whom thou hast given me, be with me where I am; that they may behold my glory, which thou hast given me."*

John 17 is a high priestly prayer of Christ to the Father for a chosen few. Those were given to Him to redeem. Those given to Christ will without fail be brought to a saving faith in Christ Jesus.

Matthew 1:21 *"And she shall bring forth a Son, and thou shalt call his name Jesus: for he shall save his people from their sins."*

Never In scripture are we told that Jesus died for all of humanity. But rest assured, all of those Christ did die for either are or will be saved.

Should you be one of those given to Christ you need to know that you were purchased with a price, the shed blood of Christ, and that you are not your own.

I Corinthians 6:19-20 *"What? Know ye not that your body is the temple of the Holy Ghost which is in you, which ye have of God, and ye are not your own. (20) For ye are bought with a price: therefore glorify God in your body, and in your spirit, which are God's."*

The underlying question is, if you are not now saved are you one of those given to Christ by the Father to save? Sobering thought.

CHAPTER 5

Total Hereditary Depravity of all Mankind

To fail to understand the Bible doctrine of hereditary depravity and the work of the Spirit in salvation is to fail in every way in the understanding of the way of salvation and all that pertains to the Christian life.

To fail in this point is like a surveyor failing to get the right starting point in the survey of a plot of land. The surveyor must start at the right place or the whole survey will be wrong.

The doctrine of the depravity of the human race is fundamental. If you are wrong in this doctrine—all else will be wrong. The following pages give what the Bible teaches, and the student should become as familiar with the Scriptures on this subject as he is with the multiplication table or the alphabet. Everything depends on a correct understanding of this doctrine.

Biblical terminology

Those redeemed

Salvation, heirs of God, saved, redeemed, born again, regenerated, the righteous, quickened, the elect, children of God, sheep, in Christ, the new man. All of these have been redeemed by Jesus Christ, have the pardon of sin, and have eternal life.

Those not redeemed

Children of the devil, unregenerate, unsaved, the wicked, the natural man, the wrath of God presently abiding on them, the non-elect, goats, those in the flesh, the old man, carnal are examples of undegenerated man.

The non-elect will never know the glories of Christ, or His gospel. They will retain their natural man status, and will forever be lost and the wrath of God presently and forever abides on them.

The elect are those who have been given to Christ to be redeemed from the world, and have already been saved, or will be saved at the appointed time.

Total inherited depravity

- TOTAL—entire person, body, mind, and soul. Every facet of man is corrupted.
- DEPRAVITY—evil continually, inherited from Adam. A tendency to sin by nature.

Man is totally depraved in the sense that he has no love for God, and his nature is completely opposed to God.

This sinful nature we inherited from Adam. God created Adam perfect, but under voluntary transgression, fell from this holy estate, and received a nature completely opposed to God. That sinful nature has been passed down to the present day to all mankind.

Romans 3:19 *"Now we know that what things soever the law saith, it saith to them who are under the law: that every mouth may be stopped, and all the world may become guilty before God."*

David said in Psalms 51:5 *"Behold, I was shaped and in iniquity; and in sin did my mother conceive me."*

Psalm 58:3 *"The wicked are estranged from the womb: they go astray as soon as they be born, speaking lies."*

This means man is not a free moral agent. He is in bondage to sin from conception and is altogether hopeless and helpless outside of the grace and mercy of God. There is nothing he can or would do to lift himself up to a holy God.

Jeremiah 13:23 *"Can the Ethiopian change his skin, or the leopard his spots? then may he also do good, that are accustomed to do evil."*

Ephesians 2:3 *"Among whom also we all had our conversation in times past in the lusts of our flesh, fulfilling the desires of the flesh and of the mind; and were by nature the children of wrath, even as others."*

We aren't sinners because we sin, on the contrary. We sin because were sinners. A lion cub doesn't become a lion only after he makes his first kill, or eats its first morsel of meat. He's born a lion, and there's nothing he can do to change that. Asking a sinner to become a Christian is like asking a lion to become a vegetarian. It's contrary to his nature. This also means babies aren't born innocent as many believe. They are born with a sinful nature that will rule their lives and cause them to be destitute of anything good in the eyes of God.

Romans 8:7-8 *"Because the carnal mind is enmity against God: for it is not subject to the law of God, neither indeed can be. (8) So then they that are in the flesh cannot please God."*

Jeremiah 17:9 *"The heart is deceitful above all things, and desperately wicked: who can know it?"*

Isaiah 64:6 *"But we are all as an unclean thing, and all our righteousnesses are as filthy rags; and we all do fade as a leaf and our iniquities, like the wind, have taken us away."*

Our righteousnesses are the very best we have to offer, and are burned in a heap of filthy rags. Many live their lives volunteering in hospitals, nursing homes, shelters for the homeless etc. to no avail. They only lack one thing "faith in Jesus Christ". All their good deeds will go unrewarded.

Romans 8:8 *"So then they that are in the flesh cannot please God."*

Hebrews 11:6 *"But without faith it is impossible to please him: for he that cometh to God must believe that he is, and that he is a rewarder of them that diligently seek him."*

Hell will be filled with so-called good, moral, upstanding, taxpaying citizens. They only lack faith in Jesus Christ. They mistake head knowledge for faith. Just to know Jesus Christ isn't to trust in Him. Recognizing Christ's name isn't being in Christ. We must have an abiding relationship with Him. There must be a longing for Him, and a desire to be with Him, and to serve Him.

Matthew 7:21-23 *"Not every one that saith unto me, Lord, Lord, shall enter into the kingdom of heaven; but he that doeth the will of my Father which is in heaven. (22) Many will say to me in that day, Lord, Lord, have we not prophesied in thy name? and in thy name have cast out devils? and in thy name done many wonderful works? (23) And then will I profess unto them, I never knew you: depart from me, ye that work iniquity."*

Total inherited depravity doesn't mean man is as evil as he could be. Just that every faculty of man is corrupt, mind, body and soul. The entire or total man is bad by nature. Man is totally devoid of any love of God. He is estranged from God and has no desire to ever be reconciled to Him.

Romans 8:7 *"Because the carnal mind is enmity against God: for it is not subject to the law of God, neither indeed can be."*

I Corinthians 2:14 *"But the natural man receiveth not the things of the Spirit of God: for they are foolishness unto him: neither can he know them, because they are spiritually discerned."*

Man naturally speaking is opposed to any and all things spiritual, and is completely unable within him to ever come to Christ for salvation. The natural man is spiritually dead and must be quickened spiritually by the Holy Spirit before he can or would desire a close relationship with God.

Therefore man is completely hopeless and helpless of ever being reconciled to God, except God comes to him and grants to him everything necessary to his salvation. That means those who are sons of God are saved by God's grace (Unmerited favor). Salvation then is wholly of God with no merits from man.

> Romans 6:23 *"For the wages of sin is death; but the gift of God is eternal life through Jesus Christ our Lord."*

We've heard it said "in the best of people there's a little bit of bad, and in the worst of people lies a little bit of good." On the earthly side this may have a ring of truth, but spiritually speaking this is not true. Also the question is asked, "Why do bad things happen to good people?" The truth of that question is there are no good people. There is none good, no not one, Jesus said.

If it were not through the mercy and grace of God, this world would open up and all of humanity would fall headlong into hell. The lake of fire is the only just and fitting place for lost man to reap his just deserts. Man's whole being is depraved. That is his mind, body, and soul is corrupt. His nature is only evil continually, and is completely unable and unwilling to come to a loving God for reconciliation.

That makes this subject the most important and valuable subject you'll ever encounter.

Lost man is by nature spiritually dead and is in need of the Holy Spirit to quicken (make alive) him spiritually. The soul and spirit are then born of God, and receive eternal life. The body however does not. It will continue to sin for it is the flesh and retains its evil inclinations.

> Galatians 5:16-17 *"This I say then, Walk in the Spirit, and ye shall not fulfill the lust of the flesh. For the flesh lusteth against the Spirit, and the Spirit against the flesh: and these are contrary the one to the other: so that ye cannot do the things that ye would."*

I Corinthians 9:27 *"But I keep under my body, and bring it into subjection: lest that by any means, when I have preached to others, I myself should be a cast away."*

There is a continual warfare raging in the life of a child of God. The flesh is still opposed to the things of the spirit of God, and the newly born spirit within man is seeking only to please and serve Christ. Those of us who have been saved by the Grace of God through faith in Jesus Christ seek only to serve Christ. But God didn't save the flesh. The flesh remains the same and will one day pay the ultimate price of death for sin. Therefore we must as Paul said, bring the body (flesh) under subjection. Notice what the Apostle Paul says concerning this.

Romans 7:15-25 *"For that which I (the flesh) do I (the spirit) allow not: for what I (flesh) would, that do I (spirit) not; but what I (flesh) hate, that do I (spirit). (16) If then I (flesh) do that which I (spirit) would not, I (spirit) consent unto the law that it is good. (17) Now than it is no more I (spirit) that do it, but sin that dwelleth in me. (18) For I (spirit) know that in me (that is, in my flesh,) dwelleth no good thing: for to will is present with me; but how to perform that which is good I find not. (19) For the good that I (spirit) would I (flesh) do not: but the evil which I (spirit) would not, that I (flesh) do. (20) Now for if I (flesh) do that I (spirit) would not, it is no more I (spirit) that do it, but sin that dwelleth in me. (21) I find then a law, that, when I would do good, evil is present with me. (22) For I delight in the law of God after the inward man: (23) But I see another law in my members, warring against the law of my mind, and bringing me into captivity to the law of sin which is in my members. (24) O wretched man that I am! Who shall deliver me from the body of this death? (25) I thank God through Jesus Christ our Lord. So then with the mind I myself serve the law of God; but with the flesh the law of sin."* (Emphasis mine, for clarification only L.D.)

For the child of God in this world, the warfare rages on, but the ultimate victory will be won.

Romans 8:1 *"THERE IS therefore now no condemnation to them which are in Christ Jesus, who walk not after the flesh, but after the Spirit."* (Emphasis mine L.D.)

Following is a list of scriptural necessities of salvation. Notice while listing these, the one thing they all have in common. They are all given by and performed by God only, and not by man.

1. A nature change.

    I Corinthians 2:14 *"But the natural man receiveth not the things of the Spirit of God: for they are foolishness unto him: neither can he know them, because they are spiritually discerned."*

    Romans 8:7-8 *"Because the carnal mind is enmity against God: for it is not subject to the law of God, neither indeed can be. (8) So then they are in the flesh cannot please God."*

    Ephesians 2:1-6 *"and you hath he quickened who were dead in trespasses and sins; (2) Wherein in time past ye walked according to the course of this world, according to the prince of the power of the air, the spirit that now worketh in the children of disobedience: (3) Among whom also we all had our conversation in times past in the lusts of our flesh, fulfilling the desires of the flesh and of the mind; and were by nature the children of wrath, even as others. (4) But God, who is rich in mercy, for his great love wherewith he loved us, (5) Even when we were dead in sins, hath quickened us together with Christ, (by grace ye are saved) (6) And hath raised us up together, and made us sit together in heavenly places in Christ Jesus:"*

The natural man is a spiritual corpse. He is dead, and unable to come to Christ. He must be made alive spiritually before any move toward Christ can be made. He must be drawn by Christ.

John 6:44 *"No man can come to me, except the Father which hath sent me draw him: and I will raise him up at the last day."*

Ezekiel 11:19-20 *"And I will give them one heart, and I will put a new spirit within you; and I will take the stony heart out of their flesh, and will give them an heart of flesh: (20) That they may walk in my statues, and keep mine ordinances, and do them: and they shall be my people, and I will be their God."*

This is Gods doing upon man, not man upon himself.

2. <u>Love of God</u>.

Romans 5:5 *"And hope maketh not ashamed; because the love of God is shed abroad in our hearts by the Holy Ghost which is given unto us."*

Without this work of the Holy Spirit man will forever be an enemy of God.

3. <u>Faith in Jesus Christ</u>

Romans 12:3 *"for I say, through the grace given unto me, to every man that is among you, not to think of himself more highly than he ought to think; but to think soberly, according as God hath dealt to every man the measure of faith."*

It is God's choice to whom he gives faith and even the measure of faith to each of his elect as only he chooses.

4. <u>Godly sorrow or conviction of sins</u>.

II Corinthians 7:9-10 *"Now I rejoice, not that ye were made sorry, but that ye sorrowed to repentance: for ye were made sorry after a godly manner, that ye might receive damage by us in nothing. (10) For godly sorrow worketh repentance to salvation not to be repented of: but the sorrow of the world worketh death."*

Godly sorrow is God convicting you of your sins. That's when you realize your sinfulness and your unworthiness of ever coming to Christ for forgiveness. This godly sorrow works toward repentance.

Acts 11:18 *"When they heard these things, they held their peace, and glorified God, saying, Then hath God also to the Gentiles granted repentance unto life."*

Luke 13:3 Jesus speaking, *"I tell you, nay: but, except ye repent, ye shall all likewise perish."*

Repentance is not a necessity to salvation, but evidence of salvation. Any profession of faith not accompanied with repentance is a hollow profession and meaningless.

6. Personal choice.

Philippians 2:13 *"For it is God which worketh in you both to will and to do of his good pleasure."*

Man must make a choice to be a Christian, but left to him this would never happen. Only when the Godhead comes unto a lost sinner and gives him or her everything needful for salvation can one make this choice. This is regeneration.

John 6:37-39 Jesus speaking, *"All that the Father giveth me shall come to me; and him that cometh to me I will in no wise cast out. (38) For I came down from heaven, not to do mine own will, but the will of him that sent me. (39) And this is the Father's will which hath sent me, that of all which he hath given me I should lose nothing, but should raise it up again at the last day."*

These are all gifts of God given to a certain innumerable multitude, chosen only by God without anything seen or foreseen in them. It's just simply His choice or his election.

Romans 9:11 *"For the children being not yet born, neither having done any good or evil, that the purpose of God according to election might stand, not of works, but him that calleth;"*

Ephesians 1:4-5 & 11 *"According as he hath chosen use in him before the foundation of the world, that we should be holy and without blame before him in love: (5) Having predestinated us unto the adoption of children by Jesus Christ to himself, according to the good pleasure of his will. (11) In whom also we have obtained an inheritance, being predestinated according to the purpose of him who worketh all things after the counsel of his own will."*

In short, God has from before the foundation of the world, chosen a certain innumerable multitude to salvation through Jesus Christ our Lord. Those who are the chosen were given to Christ to redeem through his shed blood on the cross at Calvary.

John 15:16 Jesus said, *"Ye have not chosen me, but I have chosen you."*

God the Father gave to God the Son a multitude of sinners to save from the penalty of sin, and to grant eternal life.

John 17:2 *"As thou hast given him power over all flesh, that he should give eternal life to as many as thou hast given him."*

John 17:6; 9 and 11 *"I have manifested thy name unto the men which thou gavest me out of the world: thine they were, and thou gavest them me; and they have kept thy word."(9) "I pray for them: I pray not for the world, but for them which thou hast given me; for they are thine." (11) And now I am no more in the world, but these are in the world, and I come to thee. Holy*

Father, keep through thine own name those whom thou hast given me, that they may be one, as we are."

I stand as a child of God by faith in Jesus Christ, faith that was granted to me by the Father. Everything needful for my salvation was given to me. Nothing earned or deserved.

Ephesians 2:8-9 *"For by grace are ye saved through faith; and that not of yourselves: it is the gift of God: (9) Not of works, lest any man should boast."*

Total inherited depravity means all mankind is under the condemnation of a just God, rightfully condemned because of his sinful nature. Sin must always pay the dreadful price of death. Were it not for a merciful and gracious God all of humanity would be condemned to the outer reaches of hell.

Understand now the plan of salvation God decreed through His Son Jesus Christ. Christ was sent to pay the full price of sin through his death on the cross. All the sins of all those given to Christ by the Father were laid on Christ while on the cross and in His death the price was paid. God the Father was satisfied with the shed blood of Christ and the payment for sin was paid in full. Christ became our propitiation (substitute) and died in our place.

Romans 3:25 *"Whom God hath set forth to be a propitiation through faith in his blood, to declare his righteousness for the remission of sins that are past, through the forbearance of God;"*

Christ took my sins upon him to pay the uttermost penalty, and gave to me his righteousness. Therefore my sins are gone and Christ's righteousness is declared by God to my charge.

II Corinthians 5:21 *"For he hath made him to be sin for us, who knew no sin; that we might be made the righteousness of God in him."*

I am not righteous but I am declared righteous by God the Father through faith in Jesus Christ our Lord.

CHAPTER 6

Saving Faith

Ephesians 2:8 *"For by grace are ye saved through faith; and that not of yourselves: it is the gift of God:"*

God's Grace

For by grace or simply stated because of God's grace. If not for the attribute of God's grace, all mankind would be doomed to the outer reaches of hell. Grace means unmerited and undeserved favor of God. It means man only deserves, and earns complete condemnation. It means, God loves, and bestows blessings on men who are deserving of just the opposite of what He gives them. It means there is no cause within man for God to love or embrace them.

Romans 3:24 *"Being justified freely by his grace through the redemption that is in Christ Jesus:"*

"Freely" means without a cause, and by, or because of God's grace. God justifies us without a cause within ourselves.

Romans 9:11 *"For the children being not yet born, neither having done any good or evil, that the purpose of God according to election might stand, not of works, but of him that calleth:"*

There is nothing seen or foreseen within us for God to love or redeem. Simply because God chose us for Himself and within Himself before the creation of the world; God also chose the avenue of faith given to us by Christ to justify us.

Saving Faith

God chose faith as the avenue to justify those whom Christ died for. *"For by grace are ye saved through faith"* Yet what is faith? It's been said that faith is merely trusting in and having confidence in. But I think it's much more than that. We usually have a confidence in our automobile that when we turn the key the engine will start. This confidence or faith is not a saving faith. This faith is a faith from within ourselves, and is not the faith of Christ.

We are saved because of God's grace and through a saving faith that is not of ourselves. It's not a faith coming from within ourselves. *"It is the gift of God."* The "it" is referring to faith. So faith doesn't come from within us, but comes from God, and is a gift from God to us.

Hebrews 12:2 *"Looking unto Jesus the author and finisher of our faith;"*

This clearly shows that saving faith originates, not within us, but within Christ. It comes to us from Christ as a gift. Secondly this verse tells of Christ's keeping us by the same faith that saved us. Christ is both the author (originator) and finisher (sustainer) of our faith in Christ.

Philippians 1:6 *"Being confident of this very thing, that he which hath begun a good work in you will perform it until the day of Jesus Christ:"*

Being confident of God's truth is a very wonderful blessing from God. To be confident of what God is telling us is very reassuring and important.

Luke 1:3 *"It seemed good to me also, having had perfect understanding of all things from the very first,"*

This is being confident of Jesus continuing to keep us until and through to the day of Jesus Christ. This takes us beyond this world into the next. So how confident are you? This is a literal translation. Jesus will keep us throughout this world. How confident are you of that fact? Is your trust really in Christ that he will do this? Do you really believe Him?

The "good work" that Christ has begun is the work of saving faith. He gives it as a gift, and keeps or sustains our faith all through this life. The Day of Jesus Christ is the rapture, should you or I live that long. I find great joy in that confidence. It strengthens and encourages me.

> Galatians 2:16 *"Knowing that a man is not justified by the works of the law, but by the faith of Jesus Christ, even we have believed in Jesus Christ, that we might be justified by the faith of Christ, and not by the works of the law: for by the works of the law shall no flesh be justified."*

This is not your faith in Christ, but Christ's faith in you toward Him. It is the faith of Christ. Not merely a self-derived faith or confidence in Christ. Saving faith originates with Christ, and is given as a gift to us.

While I have not checked all the translations of today I have found the NKJV, the Amplified Bible and the NIV are incorrect in their translations. The Textus Receptus, the Geneva Bible, and the KJV are correct in their translations.

While faith in Jesus Christ is in itself correct, it does not reveal the truth of what saving faith is, nor where it originates from. Half a truth is not sufficient when the whole truth is before us.

> Romans 3:22 *"Even the righteousness of God which is by faith OF Jesus Christ unto all and upon all them that believe: for there is no difference:"* (Emphasis mine L.D.)

CHAPTER 7

Exposing the Freewill Heresy

Little argument can be made about the fact that God did predestine the vessels of honor to be saved eternally. However, the Arminian argument is that God in His foreknowledge knew beforehand who would believe, and elected them to salvation, and those that continued to reject Christ were termed vessels unto dishonor, and to be cast into the lake of fire.

In this short script I will endeavor to expose this idea as false, and of great error. This heresy raises man in his pride and places him well above the depravity the scriptures put him in. This also denigrates God to a level of man in both power and sovereignty. Man in his pride will do most anything to glorify himself even to the point of lowering God beneath or equal to himself.

> Psalm 50:21b *". . . thou thoughtest that I was altogether such as one as thyself: but I will reprove thee, and set them in order before thine eyes."*

The free agency of man says, our salvation is not wholly of God. It says we do really contribute something to our salvation. It teaches if man will through his own choice receive Christ, God will grant him eternal life. You then have somewhat to glory in. Your salvation could not have been complete without your choice to receive Christ.

Think about what you are saying and what you believe. As I have said many times before and so I say now again. "If you will think it through to the ultimate end you will change your mind" Are we saved by pure grace or aren't we? That is the ultimate question. The natural man is free to roam within the realm of his own nature but is incapable of going beyond his own nature, and his nature is anti-God. He has no desire for anything spiritual and wouldn't come if he could.

> 1 Corinthians 2:14 *"But the natural man receiveth not the things of the Spirit of God: for they are foolishness unto him: neither can he know them, because they are spiritually discerned."*

When an elect of God turns to receive Christ for salvation he does so only and purely because the Holy Spirit put that desire within him.

> Philippians 2:13 *"For it is God which worketh in you both to will and to do of his good pleasure."*

> Psalms 65:4 *"Blessed is the man whom thou choosest, and causest to approach unto thee, that he may dwell in thy courts: we shall be satisfied with the goodness of thy house, even of thy holy temple."*

> Ezekiel 36:26 *"A new heart also will I give you, and a new spirit will I put within you: and I will take away the stony heart out of your flesh, and I will give you a heart of flesh."*

Consider this as well. God is not a failure and never has been. I've heard it said so many times, "well Satan won that battle". Satan has never won a battle that God didn't give him. If Satan ever won a battle that God intended on winning, Satan would have dethroned God, and Satan would be our god. God is a sovereign God that does as He pleases, when He pleases; to whomever He pleases, and however he pleases without failure.

> Isaiah 46:10-11 *"Declaring the end from the beginning, and from ancient times the things that are not yet done, saying, My counsel shall stand, and I will do all my pleasures: (11) Calling a ravenous bird from the east, the man that executeth my counsel from a far country: yea, I have spoken it, I will also bring it to pass; I have purposed it, I will also do it."*

God has never lost a battle to Satan as many believe. God would cease to be God as Satan would dethrone Him and become our god. This is Satan's goal.

> Isaiah 14:12-14 *"How art thou fallen from heaven, O Lucifer, son of the morning! how art thou cut down to the ground, which*

*didst weaken the nations! (13) For thou hast said in thine heart,
I will ascend into heaven, I will exalt my throne above the stars
of God: I will also sit upon the mount of the congregation, in
the sides of the north: (14) I will ascend above the heights of the
clouds; I will be like the most High."*

God has never lost a single soul to Satan that He intended to rescue
from condemnation. God has vessels unto honor which are his elect from
before the foundation of this world. There are also vessels unto dishonor.
These are sinners that God leaves to their own sinful choices, and to
their own just condemnation. These were not given to Christ to redeem,
and were never in God's plan of salvation from the very beginning. This
glorifies God and humbles man. This makes God the potter and man the
clay. The vessels unto honor made by the potter have within them only
what the potter put within them. The finished vessel made by the potter is
not the choosing of the clay but only of the potter, and God is the potter.

Romans 9:11-24 *"(For the children being not yet born, neither
having done any good or evil, that the purpose of God according
to election might stand, not by works, but to him that calleth:)
(12) It was said unto her, The elder shall serve the younger. (13)
As it is written, Jacob have I loved, but Esau have I hated. (14)
What shall we say then? Is there unrighteous with God? God
forbid. (15) For he saith to Moses, I will have mercy on whom
I will have mercy, and I will have compassion on whom I will
have compassion. (16) So then it is not of him that willeth, nor
of him that runneth, but of God that sheweth mercy. (17) For the
scripture saith unto Pharaoh, Even for this same purpose have I
raised thee up, that I might shew my power in thee, and that my
name might be declared throughout all the earth. (18) Therefore
hath he mercy on whom he will have mercy, and whom he will
he hardeneth. (19) Thou wilt say then unto me Why doeth he yet
find fault? For who hath resisted his will? (20) Nay but, O man,
who art thou that repliest against God? Shall the thing formed
say to him that formed it, Why has thou made me thus? (21)
Hath not the potter power over the clay, of the same lump to*

make one vessel unto honour, and another unto dishonour? (22) What if God, willing to shew his wrath, and to make his power known, endured with much longsuffering the vessels of wrath fitted to destruction: (23) And that he might make known the riches of his glory on the vessels of mercy, which he had afore prepared unto glory. (24) Even us, whom he hath called, not of the Jews only, but also of the Gentiles?"

The greatest dividing factor that separates the two positions is the understanding, or the lack of understanding of how depraved is total depravity. If the natural man is dead spiritually, how is it he can make a spiritual move to receive Christ if he is spiritually dead? How dead is dead? How is it he can make a choice? Such a choice is completely under the realm of impossibility.

John 6:44 *"No man can come to me, except the Father which hath sent me draw him: and I will raise him up at the last day."*

John 6:65 *"And he said, Therefore said I unto you, that no man can come unto me, except it were given unto him of my Father."*

Man's nature is anti-God and spiritually dead.

Therefore he must be quickened spiritually before he can possibly ever make any decision or make a move toward Christ. The quickening of the spirit must precede anything else in our salvation experience. Our nature must be changed first.

Romans 8:7 *"Because the carnal mind is enmity against God: for it is not subject to the law of God, neither indeed can be."*

2 Corinthians 5:17-18 *"Therefore if any man be in Christ, he is a new creature: old things are passed away; behold, all things are become new. (18) And all things are of God, who hath reconciled us to himself by Jesus Christ, and hath given to us the ministry of reconciliation;"*

Two questions then must be answered. 1. Does man possess the ability to come to Christ, repent of his sins, and be saved at any moment? 2. Can a man, any man, reject the calling of Christ to salvation, until death, and be eternally lost?

Anyone who answers yes to either of these two questions has little or no understanding of the total depravity of man, or of the saving power of Christ. Christ was commissioned by the Father to redeem those to whom the Father gave him without the loss of a single soul.

John 17:12 *"While I was with them in the world, I kept them in thy name: those that thou gavest me I have kept, and none of them is lost, but the son of perdition; that the scripture might be fulfilled."*

The natural man is corrupted to the point of ruin, and is dead in trespasses and sin, and is under the yoke and bondage of sin. He cannot or would not escape if he could.

Ephesians 2:1-3 *"And you hath he quickened, who were dead in trespasses and sins; (2) Wherein in time past ye walked according to the course of this world, according to the prince of the power of the air, the spirit that now worketh in the children of disobedience: (3) Among whom also we all had our conversation in times past in the lust of our flesh, fulfilling the desires of the flesh and of the mind; and were by nature the children of wrath, even as others."*

What I am endeavoring to do is to show you the hopelessness and helplessness of the lost sinner. If any man is to be saved it must be the complete working of the Triune God. God the Father first had to choose him, God, the Son had to redeem him and the Holy Spirit had to bring it into reality. That makes our salvation wholly of God without any mixture of works from man.

Consider the restoration to life of Lazarus in John 11; Lazarus was dead and in the grave for three days when Jesus came to him. Jesus didn't ask him for a decision of whether or not he wanted to be made alive. He couldn't make a physical move just as a spiritually dead sinner could not make a spiritual move.

The very first act of the saving of a lost sinner must be the quickening of the spirit. Then the love of God is spread abroad in his heart. He is convicted of his sins which produces repentance. His nature has been changed from hating God to loving God. He is one of the elect of God, elected from before the foundation of the world.

If there is anything you have contributed to your salvation, whereby if you had not contributed it, and you wouldn't have been saved; you are adding works to your salvation.

Romans 11:5-6 *"Even so at this present time also there is a remnant according to the election of grace. (6) And if by grace, it is no more of works: otherwise grace is no more grace. But if it be of works, then it is no more grace: otherwise work is no more work."*

Thus we are totally at the mercy and grace of a sovereign God.

The second consideration is whether or not an elect sinner has the ability to reject the call of God to salvation till death, and be eternally lost and under the wrath of God.

I think most will agree that the natural man is lost and under the wrath of a just and righteous God, and awaiting his just condemnation should he remain in this possession till death.

John 3:18 *"He that believeth on him is not condemned: but he that believeth not is condemned already, because he hath not believed in the name of the only begotten Son of God."*

John 3:36 *"He that believeth on the Son hath everlasting life: and he that believeth not the Son shall not see life; but the wrath of God abideth on him."*

So we agree, the lost sinner is presently under the wrath of God, but that doesn't answer the question of whether he can refuse Christ's call to salvation.

God removes everything that would prohibit a sinner from coming, and gives everything that would cause him to want to come. He takes away the stony hardened heart that would prevent him from coming and give him a heart of flesh that would cause him to come.

Ezekiel 11:19-20 *"And I will give them one heart, and I will put a new spirit within you; and I will take the stony heart out of their flesh, and will give them an heart of flesh: (20) That they may walk in my statutes, and keep mine ordinances, and do them: and they shall be my people, and I will be their God."*

It is true that we must choose to come, but God governs that choice as well.

Philippians 2:13 *"For it is God which worketh in you both to will and to do of his good pleasure."*

Jesus promised to lose nothing, or no-one, and Christ never fails.

Saving faith is added to the sinner at the hand of God.

Ephesians 2:8 *"For by grace are ye saved through faith; and that not of yourselves: it is the gift of God:"*

What is it that is not of you, but is a gift of God?

Answer: FAITH.

Romans 12:3 *"For I say, through the grace given unto me, to every man that is among you, not to think of himself more highly than he ought to think; but to think soberly, according as God hath dealt to every man the measure of faith."*

Hebrews 12:2 "Looking unto Jesus the author and finisher of our faith;"

The love of God is added to the sinner's heart.

Romans 5:5 *"And hope maketh not ashamed; because the love of God is shed abroad in our hearts by the Holy Ghost which is given unto us."*

Conviction of our sins and Godly sorrow which produces repentance is given by the Holy Spirit.

2 Corinthians 7:9-10 *"Now I rejoice, not that ye were made sorry, but that ye sorrowed to repentance: for ye were made sorry after a godly manner, that ye might receive damage by us in nothing. (10) For godly sorrow worketh repentance to salvation not to be repented of: but the sorrow of the world worketh death."*

Everything needful to our salvation is given to the lost elect sinner. Nothing is left to chance. God will effectively bring the vilest sinner to Christ, and the stoutest heart is clay in His hand.

God, before the foundation of the world, brought a certain innumerable multitude unto salvation through Jesus Christ our Lord

TO THE PRAISE AND GLORY OF GOD!

CHAPTER 8

Election and Predestination

I know of no other Biblical truth that is more hated by men than that of election and predestination. However, I can have some sympathy for their cause as I once was numbered in their ranks. It was when the time was right that God revealed to me the blessed truths of scripture concerning election and predestination. Even then I was reluctant to receive them. It wasn't until the Holy Spirit gave to me the understanding of these truths that I cheerfully received them, and have embraced them as precious truths through this very day. Election and predestination are both self-humbling and God glorifying.

I can understand the humanistic and Arminian hatred for these truths. Their pride is hurt, their ego is offended, and their self-righteousness is crucified. The false idea of the free will of man has been disproved and man's sovereignty is cast away. Human pride is ever trying to reserve for itself a little bit of self-glory rather than give God all His due glory.

Election

While some will try to strip election from the Bible completely, still others will freely admit to its existence yet fail to grant God the right of His free choice. They insist that God merely looked into the future and saw some good in certain men and elected them on that basis. But it was Jesus himself that said, ". . . THERE IS NONE GOOD BUT ONE, THAT IS, GOD." **Matthew 19:17.** They must consider themselves as some sort of god's. This idea would make man more sovereign than God, and make God a servant of men. Perish the thought. God would be reacting to the first action of man, and man would be controlling God rather than God controlling man. I hope this really sounds repugnant to you as it really is. It is God dishonoring and man exalting. What need I say more to this?

Election is God choosing certain individuals from before the creation of the world, and bringing them to salvation through the shed blood of Jesus Christ our Lord.

Consider these scriptures:

Mark 13:20 *"And except that the Lord hath shortened those days, no flesh should be saved: but for the elects sake, WHOM HE HATH CHOSEN, he hath shortened the days."* (Emphasis mine LD)

Romans 9:11, *"(For the children being not yet born, neither having done any good or evil, that the purpose of God according to ELECTION might stand, not of works, But of him that calleth:)"* (Emphasis mine LD)

Romans 11:5-7, *"Even so then at this present time also there is a remnant according to the election of grace. 6. And if by grace, then is it no more of works: otherwise grace is no more grace. But if it be of works, then is it no more grace: otherwise work is no more work. 7. What then? Israel hath not obtained that which he seeketh for; but the election hath obtained it, and the rest where blinded."*

Ephesians 1:4-8 *"According as he hath chosen us in him before the foundation of the world, that we should be holy and without blame before him in love: 5. Having predestinated us unto the adoption of children by Jesus Christ to himself, according to the good pleasure of his will, 6. To the praise of the gory of his grace, wherein he hath made us accepted in the beloved. 7. In whom we have redemption through his blood, the forgiveness of sins, according to the riches of his grace; 8. Wherein he hath abounded toward us in all wisdom and prudence."*

Ephesians 1:11, *"In whom also we have obtained an inheritance, being predestinated according to the purpose of him who worketh all things after the council of his own will:"*

I Thessalonians 1:4-5, *"Knowing, brethren beloved, your election of God. 5. For our gospel came not unto you in word only, but also in power, and in the Holy Ghost, and in much assurance; as ye know what manner of men we were among you for your sake."*

II Thessalonians 2:13-14. *"But we are bound to give thanks alway to God for you, brethren beloved of the lord, because God hath from the beginning CHOSEN YOU TO SALVATION through sanctification of the Spirit and belief of the truth: 14. Whereunto he called you by our gospel to the obtaining of the glory of our Lord Jesus Christ."* (Emphasis mine LD)

Consider what Jesus said.

John 6:37-39, and 65. *"All that the Father giveth to me shall come to me: and him that cometh to me I will in no wise cast out. 38. For I came down from heaven, not to do mine own will, but the will of him that sent me. 39. And this is the Father's will which hath sent me, THAT OF ALL WHICH HE HATH GIVEN ME I SHOULD LOSE NOTHING, but should raise it up again at the last day."* 65. *"And he said, Therefore said I unto you, that no man can come unto me. except it were given unto him of my Father."* (Emphasis mine LD)

The elect are the chosen ones of God, and are also referred to in scripture as Christ's sheep.

John 10:14-16. *"I am the good shepherd, and know my sheep, and am known of mine.15. As the Father knoweth me, even so know I the Father: and I lay down my life for the sheep. 16. And other sheep I have, which are not of this fold: them also I must bring, and they shall hear my voice: and there shall be one fold, and one shepherd."*

To the praise and glory of God the Father I am saying that those who believe are the chosen ones of God and are his elect from before the foundation of the world. Christ's sheep are the ones of God's choosing and given to Christ to redeem.

The seventeenth chapter of John is a high priestly prayer of Christ to the Father in behalf of his sheep. This is my favorite chapter in the entire Bible.

John 17:

2. "*. . . he should give eternal life to as many as thou hast given him.*"
6. "*. . . which thou gavest me out of the world.*"
7. "*. . . whatsoever thou hast given me are of thee.*"
9. "*. . . which thou hast given me.*"
11. "*. . . those whom thou hast given me.*"
12. "*. . . and none of them is lost.*"

Here is a stern consideration for those who don't believe.

John 10:26. "*But ye believe not, because ye are not of my sheep, as I said unto you. (27) My sheep hear my voice, and I know them, and they follow me: (28) And I give unto them eternal life: and they shall never perish, neither shall any man pluck them out of my hand. (29) My Father, which gave them me, is greater than all: and no man is able to pluck them out of my Fathers hand.*"

For those who stumble at the sovereignty of God. Read some Old Testament scriptures.

Isaiah 14:27. "*For the Lord of hosts hath purposed, and who shall disannul it, and his hand is stretched out, and who shall turn it back.*"

40:22. "*It is he that sitteth upon the circle of the earth, and the inhabitants thereof are as grasshoppers; that stretcheth out the heavens as a curtain, and spreadeth them out as a tent to dwell in.*"

46:10-11. "*Declaring the end from the beginning, and from ancient times the things that are not yet done, saying, My counsel shall stand, and I will do all my pleasure: (11)Calling a ravenous bird from the east, the man that executeth my counsel from a far country: yea, I have spoken it, I will also bring it to pass; I have purposed it, I will also do it."*

55:8-11 *"For my thoughts are not your thoughts, neither are your ways my ways, saith the Lord. (9) For as the heaven are higher than the earth, so are my ways higher than your ways, and my thoughts than your thoughts. (10) For as the rain cometh down, and the snow from heaven, and returneth not thither, but water the earth, and maketh it bring forth and bud, that it may give seed to the sower, and bread to the eater: (11) So shall my word be that goeth forth out of my mouth: it shall not return unto me void, but it shall accomplish that which I please, and it shall prosper in thing whereto I send it."*

Daniel 4:35 *"And all the inhabitants of the earth are reputed as nothing: and he doeth According to his will in the army of heaven, and among the inhabitants of the earth; and none can stay his hand, or say unto him. what doest thou?*

From these precious scriptures we learn that God is a sovereign God. God does as he pleases, whenever he pleases, and to whomever he pleases, without seeking first our permission or approval. God is not obligated to anyone for anything. However, God is always true and faithful, always gracious kind and loving. The very fact that God allowed the human race to continue after the fall proves He is a gracious, loving, and kind God. God could have sent the entire human race to the depths of hell and still been gracious, loving and kind. However if He chose to rescue some and not others He is free to do so without offending any of his attributes.

Matthew 20:15. *"Is it not lawful for me to do what I will with my own? Is thine eye evil, because I am good?"*

Particular Redemption

Particular redemption (also referred to by some as limited atonement) is the scriptural teaching that Christ's sacrificial death atoned for only those to whom God the Father gave to Christ to redeem. Christ's sacrificial death and his shed blood atoned only for the elect. These are also referred to in scripture as Christ's sheep of which he is the good shepherd.

John 5:21. *"For as the Father raiseth up the dead, and quickeneth them: Even so the Son quickeneth whom He will."*

Acts 13:48c *". . . as many as were ordained to eternal life believed."*

Romans 8:28-30 *"And we know that all things work together for good to them that love God, to them who are the called according to his purpose. (29) For whom he did foreknow, he also did predestinate to be conformed to the image of his Son, that he might the first born among many brethren. (30) Moreover whom he did predestinate, them he also called: and whom he called, them he also justified; and whom he justified, them he also glorified."*

Again, God chose from before the foundation of the world a certain innumerable multitude of sinners for Christ to redeem. These are Christ's sheep of both Jew and Gentile. Christ shed his blood as our substitute paying our sin debt. He rose from the dead for our justification. Christ also died as our propitiation.

Romans 3:25-26. *"Whom God hath set forth to be a propitiation through faith in his blood, to declare his righteousness for the remission of sins that are past, through the forbearance of God: (26) To declare, I say, at this time his righteousness: that he might be just, and the justifier of him which believeth in Jesus."*

II Corinthians 5:21. *"For he hath made him to be sin for us, who knew no sin; that we might be made the righteousness of God in him."*

I John 2:1-2. *"My little children, these things write I unto you, that ye sin not. And if any man sin, we have an advocate with the Father, Jesus Christ the righteous: (2) And he is the propitiation for our sins: and not for our's only, but also for the sins of the whole world."*

The phrase "the whole world" is having reference to not only the Jews, but also to the Gentiles spread around the world. (Globe) Not necessarily every person, but every country, every nationality, every language of people on earth.

Propitiation is to appease God's wrath towards his chosen [elect] ones. Thus God is, and remains just in justifying those to whom he gave to the Son to die for. God is both just and the justifier of them who believe in Christ. God declares his elect as just, and righteous. While on the cross Christ took upon himself our sins, and charged to our account his righteousness. Therefore, we have access to God's Kingdom. We are declared righteous without God offending any of his attributes.

Christ's sacrificial death on the cross accomplished several things. First, he paid the sin debt of God's elect. Second he satisfied the wrath of God concerning our sins, past, present and future. Third, He charged to our account his righteousness that God the Father would be just and declares us as just also. In so doing Christ secured the salvation of all to whom it was intended for.

I understand that too many of the readers of this writing this is new and even shocking. This is a truth that has been neglected and even abandon from behind the pulpits today. But should you still have reservations, read Romans 8 & 9. You should begin to understand, we are called according to God's purpose, not ours.

Romans 9:13-24 *"As it is written, Jacob have I loved, but Esau have I hated. (14) What shall we say then? Is there unrighteousness with God? God forbid. (15) For he saith to Moses, I will have mercy on whom I will have mercy, and I will have compassion on whom I will have compassion. (16) So then it is not of him that willeth, nor of him that runneth, but of God that sheweth mercy. (17) For the scripture saith unto Pharaoh, Even for this same purpose have I raised thee up, that I might shew my power in thee, and that my name might be declared throughout all the earth. (18) Therefore hath he mercy on whom he will have mercy, and whom he will he hardeneth. (19) Thou wilt say then unto me, Why doth he yet find fault? For who hath resisted his will? (20) Nay but, O man, who art thou that repliest against God? Shall the thing formed say to him that formed it, Why hast thou made me thus? (21) Hath not the potter power over the clay, of the same lump to make one vessel unto honour, and another unto dishonour? (22) What if God, willing to shew his wrath, and to make his power known, endured with much longsuffering the vessels of wrath fitted to destruction: (23) And that he might make known the riches of his glory on the vessels of mercy, which he had afore prepared unto glory, (24) Even us, whom he hath called, not of the Jews only, but also of the Gentiles?"*

The human race is clay in the hands of God, and he is the potter. Should the clay instruct the potter of what to make of it? A woodcraftsman picks up a piece of wood and chooses what he will make of it. He may choose to make a waste basket to hold trash, or he may choose to make a beautiful piece of furniture. The choice is his. So it is with God and the human race. To one he will make a vessel of honor and to another a vessel of dishonor. Whatever his choice may be he will receive his due honor and glory from it. The Pharaoh was clay in God's hands and God had a purpose which he achieved, and God was glorified through him even though he was a vessel unto dishonor.

Let this be noted here that what I am about to say is my opinion as I cannot prove this with the scriptures. "God need not ever create or cause anyone to be a vessel unto dishonor. All mankind are born as vessels of dishonor from the fall of man in the Garden of Eden to the present day. All mankind are sinful and unclean by nature, and are all born as vessels of dishonor from their mother's womb. God merely takes his elect and redeems them through the shed blood of Christ. The non-elect through Adam are born as vessels of dishonor, and left to themselves are doomed to eternity without God in just condemnation of their willful sins."

To many the question must then be asked. Why God did chose some and not others, or what is the deciding factor of who the elect is and who is not? To this we can only answer as the Apostle Paul answered to the church at Ephesus. Ephesians 1:5c "... *ACCORDING TO THE GOOD PLEASURE OF HIS WILL.*" Evidently God didn't feel obligated to answer that question. It was and is in His own heart and in His own mind to do as he pleases. We do know that it wasn't because of any good seen or foreseen in us as there is no good within us.

Romans 9:11. "*(For the children being not yet born, neither having done any good or evil, that the purpose of God according to election might stand, not of works, but of him that calleth:)*"

If God looked down through time and saw some good in us and elected us on that basis our salvation would be hinged on our works rather than through faith in Christ.

Ephesians 2:8-9. "*For by grace are ye saved through faith: and that not of yourselves: it is the gift of God: 9. Not of works, lest any man should boast.*"

Titus 3:5. "*Not by works of righteousness which we have done, but according to his mercy he saved us, by the washing of regeneration, and the renewing of the Holy Ghost.*"

Man is corrupt from his mother's womb, and is in no-way deserving of God's favor upon him. Therefore God created a plan of salvation that would bypass all of man's inabilities and through grace supply all the spiritual needs of the elect. Thus our salvation is wholly of God, and not of man.

To understand the total and complete depravity of man is to understand the complete ruin of man. We are therefore forced to cast aside any idea that God foresaw any good in us to use as a basis to elect us. There can therefore be no boasting on our part.

Understanding also that man cannot, nor ever could have chosen Christ. His nature would have prevented him from ever reaching out to Christ for salvation. He is alienated from Christ and is at enmity with Christ. Any and everything man will ever receive from God in salvation comes directly from God, and only by God's choosing.

John 3:27. *"John answered and said, A man can receive nothing, except it be given him from heaven."*

John 6:44. *"No man can come to me, except the father which hath sent me draw him: and I will raise him up at the last day."*

Romans 8:7. *"Because the carnal mind is enmity against God: for it is not subject to the law of God, neither indeed can be."*

I Corinthians 2:14. *"But the natural man receiveth not the things of the Spirit of God: for they are foolishness unto him: neither can he know them, because they are spiritually discerned."*

There is nothing we can do to cause Christ to save us. We are at the mercy of God. All the credit, glory, and honor goes to the triune God. God the Father chose me, and planned my salvation. God the Son paid the price to redeem me. God the Holy Ghost brought about and executed my salvation. All the praise is his, and like King David declared in PSALMS 116:12. "WHAT SHALL I RENDER UNTO THE LORD FOR ALL HIS BENEFITS TOWARD ME?"

Regeneration is the Holy Spirit working out my salvation, and will ultimately conform me to the image of Christ. He gives me spiritual and eternal life. He removes the scales from my eyes that I may discern spiritual matters, reveals my sinful condition and my pending doom. He grants me repentance by giving me a Godly sorrow for my sins. He sheds abroad in my heart an unquenchable love for God. Everything needful in my salvation is given by the Holy Spirit including a personal choice of receiving Christ as my Savior.

Philippians 2:13. *"For it is God which worketh in you both to will and to do of his good pleasure."*

At the point of regeneration I was started on a life long journey that will culminate at the end of my earthly life and transforms me to the image of Christ.

I John 3:2, *"Beloved, now are we the sons of God, and it doth not yet appear what we shall be: but we know that, when he shall appear, we shall be like him, for we shall see him as he is."*

He took away my heart of stone and gave me a heart of flesh. He then shed abroad in my heart a real love for God.

Romans 5:5b *". . . the love of God is shed abroad in our hearts by the Holy Ghost which is given to us."*

The very faith in Christ that saves us is a gift from Christ.

Hebrews 12:2a, *"Looking unto Jesus the author and finisher of our faith;"*

Every aspect of our salvation is a result of the workings of a triune God. This humbles us, but exalts, and glorifies God.

It's been said to me that I'm making God out to be a glory seeking God. Well, I guess I am, and that's okay because he is all glorious. It's wrong for us to seek our own glory. Not only are we not glorious, but are sinners. We are nothing and God is everything.

Our worship of God is directly linked to what you think of yourself, and what you think God to be.

Psalms 50:21b. "*. . . thou thoughtest that I was altogether such an one as thyself.*"

Our worship of God is directly linked to our view of what we are and what God is. It's important to get them both right. Apostle Paul had it right when he said "*. . . BY THE GRACE OF GOD I AM WHAT I AM:*" I Corinthians 15:10

CHAPTER 9

The Church that Jesus Built

A thought provoking question

T wo facts no man can deny. Jesus built His own church and no one else's, and no one else could ever build His church.

The Church Jesus Built

Matthew 16:18-19, *"And I say also unto thee, That thou art Peter, and upon this rock I will build my church; and the gates of hell shall not prevail against it. (19) And I will give unto thee the keys of the kingdom of heaven: and whatsoever thou shalt bind on earth shall be bound in heaven: and whatsoever thou shalt loose on earth shall be loosed in heaven.*

During Jesus' fleshly walk on earth, He instituted His church. This scripturally cannot be denied. This truth compels me to write this short script. From this truth, we must conclude Jesus built His church and no other church, and no one else could build His church. Try, as you may you cannot get around these facts. Jesus did not tell us where these would be, or how plentiful they would become, only that His church would be here on earth.

Our Lord also promised us that His church would never cease to exist on earth from the time He instituted it until the time He takes it up to be with him. (The rapture) *"The gates of Hades shall not prevail against it."* The promise is, it would never die or cease to exist on earth during this time. This is the perpetuity of the church.

The church that Jesus built continues to be a thorn in Satan's side, and Satan knows he cannot stop it. This however does not mean he has no tools in his arsenal to fight against it. He is relentless in his efforts to hinder, discredit, or hide it from God's elect. One of Satan's attacks on Christ's church is to counterfeit it with false churches. Churches built by man are subject to the inabilities of man and the craftiness of Satan.

II Corinthians 11:14 *"And no marvel; for Satan himself is transformed into an angel of light."* He is an arch deceiver, a slanderer of saints, oppressor of the righteous, a tempter, sower of tares, a liar, blinder of eyes of the unbelievers, etc., etc. Any way he can hinder the church Jesus built is not beneath his character. II Corinthians 2:11 *"Lest Satan should get an advantage of us: for we are not ignorant of his devices."* Many of God's elect are ignorant of Satan's devices and fall into the snare of the devil. One of these snares remains with his counterfeiting the church that Jesus built.

We know from our text that Jesus is the founder of His church, and none other. Ephesians 5:23b *". . . even as Christ is the head of the church: and he is the saviour of the body."* This makes Jesus both head and founder of His church.

Also in our text, Jesus built only one type of church. The word "church" is translated from the Greek word "ecclesia", which means a called out assembly of believers for a particular purpose or a local, visible assembly of baptized believers. Jesus called this His ecclesia (church). Any other type of church is not His church, but in effect are counterfeit churches. It is not my attempt in this writing to prove what is or is not a scriptural baptism, or the fact that baptism is essential to membership in Christ's church, another time perhaps. Sufficient for now is to show the true and only church that Jesus built is a local and visible church which He left here on earth and will one day in the future receive her up unto himself in the rapture.

In Satan's attempt to counterfeit the church that Jesus built, he introduced a new concept of a church, namely a universal concept of the church. This idea is in direct contradiction of a local church. This universal church puts all of its members into one worldwide body called the Catholic (Universal) Church. Jesus design of his church (a local church) places each church into a separate body. Thus, each scriptural church is separate from every other scriptural church and each church a separate body from all other bodies. Constantine who initiated this new concept founded this universal church. This new concept began in about the third century after Christ initiated His local church. This was the only way the Church of Rome could justify its existence. This Church of Rome was distinctly different from the church that Jesus built. It was a clever counterfeit by Satan. This church encompassed many if not all of the practices that came from Babylon. She only changed the names of the participants and practices to protect the guilty. This subject could produce much more, but this should suffice for now.

Another clever counterfeit concept from Satan is the new idea of an invisible church. All believers worldwide will make up one body or one invisible church. This is in direct conflict with the concept of the local visible body of the church that Jesus built. This new idea was to justify the existence of the Protestant churches. These were also distinctively different from the church that Jesus built, or even the Church of Rome that Constantine built. All Protestant churches came from its mother church of Rome and have no connection to the church that Jesus built.

The universal church and the invisible church have its origin by someone other than Christ, and at a time other than during Christ's lifetime here on earth. These truths should ring clearly and loudly in our ears, and cause us to flee from manmade churches and run to the church that has Jesus as its author, its head and its founder. Here it can be rightly stated that any church holding to a universal body or an invisible body is not the Lord's church, and is at best a counterfeit church having mere man as its head and founder.

Noteworthy, neither a universal church nor an invisible church can operate as a local church. Neither a universal nor invisible church can sit and partake of the Lord's Supper. Only a local body can do this. They make a mockery of baptism. The claim is you automatically become members of a worldwide invisible church when saved. Baptism is then unnecessary and unimportant. In addition, the Bride of Christ comes out of this invisible church so membership in a local church is unimportant. A universal or invisible church cannot exercise church discipline as taught by Christ in Matthew 18:15-17 *"Moreover if thy* *brother shall trespass against thee, go and tell him his fault between thee and him alone: if he shall hear thee, thou hast gained thy brother. (16) But if he will not hear thee, then take with thee one or two more, that in the mouth of two or three witnesses every word may be established. (18) And if he shall neglect to hear them, <u>tell it unto the church: but if he neglects to hear the church,</u> let him be unto thee as a heathen man and a publican."* Only in a local church can the gospel be proclaimed and defended. The local church concept that Jesus built is the only complete concept of a true church. Further, it is claimed that all believers (making up one body of Christ) is the only true church. That presupposes that the church Jesus built is not the true church. God forbid.

Scripture gives us another revelation of the church Jesus built.

II Corinthians 11:2-4 "For I am jealous over you with godly jealousy: for I have espoused you to one husband, that I may present you as a chaste virgin to Christ. (3) But I fear, lest by any means, as the serpent beguiled Eve through his subtilty, so your minds should be corrupted from the simplicity that is in Christ. (4) For if he that cometh preacheth another Jesus, whom we have not preached, or if ye receive another spirit, which ye have not received, or another gospel, which ye have not accepted, ye might well bear with him."

The church that Jesus built is espoused to Christ. That is she is Christ's espoused bride. Ephesians 5:27 *"That he might present it to himself a glorious church, not having spot, or wrinkle, or any such thing; but that it should be holy and without blemish."* The church that Jesus built is espoused (as a chaste virgin) to Christ, and will one day after she is raptured be presented to Christ as His Bride. As the serpent deceived Eve, Satan has deceived many of God's elect into following "another spirit", and "another gospel" which the disciples did not receive. II Timothy 3:5 *"Having a form of godliness, but denying the power thereof: from such turn away."* These counterfeit churches sound and seem impressive, but they preach another gospel. Paul told the churches at Galatia Galatians 1:6-9 *"I marvel that ye are so soon removed from him that called you into the grace of Christ unto another gospel: (7) Which is not another; but there be some that trouble you, and would pervert the gospel of Christ. (8) But though we, or an angel from heaven, preach any other gospel unto you than that which we have preached unto you, let him be accursed (9) As we said before, so say I now again, if any man preach any other gospel unto you than that ye have received, let him be accursed."* The new universal Church of Rome ascribed to a new gospel never taught by Christ or his disciples. Doctrines never before taught or practiced except those rescued from Babylon the Great. The practices that brought God's wrath down upon Babylon, God's people should reject all practices originating from Babylon. Any gospel or doctrine that cannot be proved in Holy writ should not be taught. Ephesians 4:14 *"That we henceforth be no more children, tossed to and fro, and carried about with every wind of doctrine, by the sleight of men, and cunning craftiness, whereby they lie in wait to deceive;"* Acts 20:29-30 *"For I know this, that after my departing shall grievous wolves enter in among you, not sparing the flock. Also of your own selves shall men arise, speaking perverse things, to draw away disciples after them."* The fears of the Apostles came true.

This is not to say that all members of the Catholic or Protestant churches are all evil unregenerate people. On the contrary, some of God's own elect abide in them. They have been deceived and have fallen into the snare of the devil. In these counterfeit churches some are saved, regenerated saints of God. These are all heaven bound (not all but some). These will be raptured and spend eternity with Christ. However, these are not Christ's bride. These will be guests at the marriage of Christ to His Bride. However, a special blessing awaits those who have joined and been faithful to the church that Jesus built.

Another false but very popular notion is that the birth of the church was on the day of Pentecost. This day of course was 50 days after Christ was crucified and 10 days after Christ ascended to sit at the right hand of the Father. Therefore, Christ was not on earth to build His church during this time. Remember Christ built His church during His earthly ministry. Many infallible proofs can be given to prove this.

This proves this notion to be false, and those churches claiming their birth on the day of Pentecost also to be false churches.

Conclusion

Jesus founded His church during His earthly visit. Therefore, any church whose origin goes back to anyone or any time other than Christ. Such as Catholic, Protestant, Pentecostal, etc. simply cannot be a scriptural church or the church that Jesus built.

Paul told the church at Ephesus in Ephesians 3:21 *"unto Him be glory in the church."* Therefore, we cannot glorify Christ outside of His church.

CHAPTER 10

The Gospel and the Baptist

First, it's important to understand Jesus did not give His church a title or denominational name. This was added some fifteen hundred years later. This came about not only by uninspired men, but also by the enemies of Christ's church. Jesus called His church "my assembly" or "my congregation". Even the word "church" is a mistranslation. What Jesus built was an assembly of regenerated (saved) saints that were baptized by John the Baptist. Jesus called out these saints to be His (Ekklesia) congregation. Thus Jesus Church is a called out assembly called to a local gathering or assembly.

Notice what Jesus said:

Matthew 16:18-19 *"And I say also unto thee, That thou art Peter, and upon this rock I will build my church; and the gates of hell shall not prevail against it. And I will give unto thee the keys of the kingdom of heaven: and whatsoever thou shalt bind on earth shall be bound in heaven: and whatsoever thou shalt loose on earth shall be loosed in heaven."*

The word *"hell"* in verse 18 is better translated as *"Hades"* which is an unseen realm of the dead. That is to say, the church Jesus built will never die, or be destroyed on earth. She (Christ's church) was left here on earth to proclaim the blessed gospel. She will remain here until Christ comes to receive her unto himself at the rapture during the last days. While on earth she is entrusted with the precious gospel, and is also espoused to Christ as His Bride.

The Gospel

While on earth Christ entrusted His church with the Gospel. She was to nurture, proclaim, and protect it. She has been doing just that for the last two thousand years. However, it's been a rough road. Millions of saints have been slain and martyred during the dark ages. Their martyrdom has been marked in a trail of blood. Hundreds of churches were completely destroyed because they would not forsake the gospel nor yield to her enemy, the church of the seven hilled city in Rome, this being the Catholic Church. The Church of Rome, later aided by the protestant churches during the reformation period, sought to completely annihilate and destroy the church Jesus built from off the earth. However, Christ promised His church that this would never happen. Even though Christ's churches were then very numerous they were decreased in number many times over. And sad as it is, some of Christ's churches falter and failed in preserving the gospel. Some caved in to the Catholic and protestant churches out of fear. They yielded to the pressures of the Roman church and lost their claim as a scriptural church, these were referred to as pseudo or irregular churches. Although Christ promised that there would always be true churches that would remain true to the gospel and their head Jesus Christ. There always has been, and until Christ comes in yonder sky there will continue to be true churches faithful to Christ. Today these churches are few in number, but they are here still being faithful with the gospel message Christ entrusted them with.

Baptist History

On the on-set of this writing I made mention of the fact that Christ did not give His church a name or a denominational title. For the first four hundred years and beyond His churches were called either by the name of their pastor or by their location, names such as" Montanists"," Novationists", Puritans, Paulicans, Arnoldists, Henricians, Waldenses, etc. It wasn't until around the fourth century that the Catholics began to refer to her as Ana-Baptists or re-baptizers because she would not accept alien infant baptism of the Catholic Church. All new converts from the Church of Rome must be re-baptized before membership in Christ church. Many years later the Ana-Baptist was shortened to Baptist.

Even though we received our name from our opposition we gladly wear it. It distinguishes us from them, and that is good. The Baptists were hated back then and still are today. Over the years the Baptist name has become very prominent in closely following the scriptures just as Jesus and the apostles taught. Thus to many it became the envy of the world. So others bearing false doctrines and false gospels took the Baptist name to themselves. They tarnished and polluted the Baptist name. So now we must conclude not every Baptist church is one of Christ's churches. This world is full of pseudo-Baptist or irregular Baptist churches that have no connection to Christ.

Hereafter, when I speak of a Baptist church I am referring not to a pseudo-Baptist church but rather a scriptural Baptist church. These are the only churches on earth that have Jesus Christ as both head and founder. She is a New Testament church because she was founded by Jesus Christ during His earthly ministry in the New Testament. Today His church is still teaching the *"whatsoever I have commanded you"*, and with the promise *"and, lo, I am with you always, even unto the end of the world. (Age) Amen."* Matthew 28:20 A Baptist is the only *"pillar and ground of the truth."* I Timothy 3:15 She is still nurturing, proclaiming and protecting the gospel of Christ that was entrusted to her. To her and only her was given the great commission. Matthew 28:19-20 (make disciples, baptize them, and teach them what Christ taught). Only the Baptists were given the ordinances of the church, (Baptism and the Lord's Supper). To her was promised the perpetuity of the church and she is the only espoused Bride of Christ. Her only head is Christ. Her only walking orders is the Bible (KJV). The Bible is a Baptist book for Baptists, by Baptists, to Baptists, and to make Baptists.

Denominationalism

Webster states: "A particular religious body with a specific name, an organization under the control of a religious denomination."

Again Jesus did not give to His church a specific name or a denominational title. This was done by those who oppose Christ's churches. This title may be a clever scheme and invention of uninspired men, but they remain unbiblical at best. Denominational headquarters are in control of their churches and have become the head of these churches rather than Christ. They are lording over God's heritage.

I Matthew 28:20 prescribes what each pastor can and cannot teach their congregations. Every denomination has an individual form of the gospel they are to teach.

We are not saying that all of these that are members of these denominations are lost, unsaved and unregenerate individuals. Indeed some are of God's elect.

Notice Revelation 18:4 *"And I heard another voice from heaven, saying, Come out of her, my people, that ye be not partakers of her sins, and that ye receive not of her plagues."*

The "my people" referred to are God's elect within them. Either these have been, are, or will be saved saints of God. These have fallen for the counterfeit churches in the world.

Salvation is by grace through faith, Ephesians 2:8-9 and not of the church as many believe. Some congregations have more saved in their membership than others.

Revelation 18:4 is an admonition to God's people to come out of them that they not partake in her evils and her plagues.

Consider also II Corinthians 6:15-18 *"And what concord hath Christ with Belial? or what part hath he that believeth with an infidel? (16) And what agreement hath the temple of God with idols? for ye are the temple of the living God; as God hath said, I will dwell in them, and walk in them; and I will be their God, and they shall be my people. (17) Wherefore come out from among them, and be ye separate, saith the Lord, and touch not the unclean thing; and I will receive you,(18) And will be a Father unto you, and ye shall be my sons and daughters, saith the Lord Almighty."*

Salvation is the first requirement of membership in one of Christ's churches. Not so with most Catholic or Protestant churches, thus making them governed by the unregenerate rather than the regenerate. How it is these can be called followers of Christ or Christian churches? Making them no better than the local P.T.A. or the Lions club.

When considering the gospel message we are told there is only one gospel and then warned to guard against those who would pervent that gospel.

Galatians 1:6-12 *"I marvel that ye are so soon removed from him that called you into the grace of Christ unto another gospel: (7) Which is not another; but there be some that trouble you, and would pervert the gospel of Christ. (8) But though we, or an angel from heaven, preach any other gospel unto you than that which we have preached unto you, let him be accursed. (9) As we said before, so say I now again, If any man preach any other gospel unto you than that ye have received, let him be accursed. (10) For do I now persuade men, or God? or do I seek to please men? for if I yet pleased men, I should not be the servant of Christ. (11) But I certify you, brethren, that the gospel which was preached of me is not after man. (12) For I neither received it of man, neither was I taught it, but by the revelation of Jesus Christ."*

Acts 20:29-31 *"For I know this, that after my departing shall grievous wolves enter in among you, not sparing the flock. (30) Also of your own selves shall men arise, speaking perverse things, to draw away disciples after them. (31) Therefore watch, and remember, that by the space of three years I ceased not to warn every one night and day with tears."*

Jude 1:4-5 *"For there are certain men crept in unawares, who were before of old ordained to this condemnation, ungodly men, turning the grace of our God into lasciviousness, and denying the only Lord God, and our Lord Jesus Christ. (5) I will therefore put you in remembrance, though ye once knew this, how that the*

Lord, having saved the people out of the land of Egypt, afterward destroyed them that believed not."

Now with these verses in mind, let me ask some all important questions. How is it that the God of all glory, a Holy, just, and righteous God, a God to whom is no variableness nor shadow of turning, James 1:17, A God that is the same yesterday, today, and forever, Hebrews 13:8 A God that is not the author of confusion. I Corinthians 14:33 Can take one true and living gospel and reshape it in fifteen different configurations to fit fifteen different denominations, and still call it one true gospel? How can this be? It can't be. It just cannot be. And shame on those who think it can be. They act to their own peril. How can it be that two or more opposing subjects that are in complete contradiction to each other be true? How can salvation by grace and salvation by works co-exist in harmony? How can a God that cannot lie have two or more sets of truths? *"Let God be true but every man a liar."* Romans 3:4

It is this very message my Baptist fore-fathers were brutally persecuted and martyred for. They gave their lives to protect the gospel. Today the gospel remains under fire by those who hate it. The persecution in America today has been greatly lessened, but it will return.

II Timothy 3:1-7 *"This know also, that in the last days perilous times shall come. (2) For men shall be lovers of their own selves, covetous, boasters, proud, blasphemers, disobedient to parents, unthankful, unholy, (3) Without natural affection, trucebreakers, false accusers, incontinent, fierce, despisers of those that are good, (4) Traitors, heady highminded, lovers of pleasures more than lovers of God; (5) Having a form of godliness, but denying the power thereof: from such turn away. (6) For of this sort are they which creep into houses, and lead captive silly women laden with sins, led away with divers lusts, (7) Ever learning, and never able to come to the knowledge of the truth."*

Matthew 24:9-14 *"Then shall they deliver you up to be afflicted, and shall kill you: and ye shall be hated of all nations for my name's sake. (10) And then shall many be offended, and shall betray one another, and shall hate one another. (11) And many false prophets shall rise, and shall deceive many. (12) And because iniquity shall abound, the love of many shall wax cold. (13) But he that shall endure unto the end, the same shall be saved. (14) And this gospel of the kingdom shall be preached in all the world for a witness unto all nations; and then shall the end come."*

Probably in our lifetime this will be fulfilled.

The gospel message is not a new one. Its two thousand years old, but few there are that have heard it.

Jesus Christ died, was buried, and rose again for a select few that were given to Christ by God the Father, from before the foundation of the world.

For this gospel we may be required to give our lives as did those before us. Our message is hated and we will be as well. Let me close with the words of Christ.

Matthew 10:28 *"And fear not them which kill the body, but are not able to kill the soul: but rather fear him which is able to destroy both soul and body in hell."*

CHAPTER 11

Distinguishing Marks of a Scriptural Church

Jesus Christ instituted His church during his public ministry on earth. And to this church he promised its perpetuity. That is, she would never cease to exist on earth from the time of her origin through to the time he came back to receive her unto himself at the first resurrection. We refer to this as the rapture of the saints.

However, man has devised counterfeit churches with unbiblical gospels and strange doctrines to replace the gospel of Christ with man pleasing doctrines aimed at satisfying the demands of the flesh. The first of these came in the third century by Constantine and is referred to as the Roman Catholic Church. Later around the fifteenth century came the reformation which produced all of the Protestant churches. Today it's difficult to distinguish the church Jesus built from all the man-made churches. It is therefore my aim to set forth some distinctive marks which will aid us in finding Christ's true church from among all the false churches of man. No copyright or patent laws could ever apply to Christ's church. Therefore we must diligently search out the scriptures. Only then can we end our quest, and identify the church that Jesus built.

Discovering Christ church can only be accomplished if we are willing to set aside all pre-conceived ideas, hatred, and bigotry and just allow scriptural truth to emerge. It is only then that we can find the one church Jesus built and will ultimately glorify Christ Eph. 3:21 *"unto Him be glory in the church by Christ Jesus throughout all ages."*

Understand also, that what I'm about to tell you, they don't want you to know; they being most of Christendom from among false churches. The revealed truth of Christ's church will take away the very reason of their existence. Such is the reason for their hatred of this truth. So much so that Christ's church was nearly stamped out of existence. This was their motivation for the persecution of Christ's church during twelve hundred years of the Dark Ages.

The New Testament Church

Matthew 16:18-19

A New Testament Church is a church that had its origin in the New Testament. Its founder is Jesus Christ and non-other. It was during Christ's earthly ministry that He said "I will build my (Ekklesia) church." Matthew 16:18. Jesus said He would and did build his church during His earthly walk on earth. It simply cannot be denied that Jesus and only Jesus is the builder of his (Ekklesia) church. Ekklesia is an assembly of called out believers to a certain locality, for a certain purpose.

This by necessity excludes all churches built by mere man many centuries later. Churches such as Catholic, Protestants and the like are the inventions of man rather than Christ.

This also means that there are no Old Testament churches. The Old Testament had the Tabernacle and the Temple. In the New Testament was the building of Christ's church.

If we are to find the church built by Jesus during the New Testament era, we must search out the scriptures to find the pattern of churches formed within the New Testament. Hebrews 8:5 says, *"Thou make all things according to the pattern shown to thee in the mount."* We are given a pattern of the church in the New Testament, and we must search it out to compare and find the true church of Jesus Christ.

Many modern day churches have a form of godliness but fall way short of the pattern given in scripture. II Timothy 3:5 *"Having a form of godliness, but denying the power thereof; from such turn away."* They may mimic the New Testament church found in scripture but they fall far short of being a scriptural, true church of Jesus Christ.

We are taught concerning the Tabernacle as well as all the furnishings within the Tabernacle, that an exact pattern of instruction had to be followed or God would not appear in the Shekinah glory over the Holy of Holies. An exact pattern had to be followed, Exodus 25:9 *"According to all that I show thee, after the pattern of the tabernacle, and the pattern of all the instruments thereof, even so shall ye make it."* No exceptions or alterations were allowed. It had to be exactly as God purposed it. So it is with Christ's church, a pattern is given to us in scripture. These patterns we refer to as distinctive marks identifying the true church of Jesus Christ.

This writing is given for the purpose of finding and identifying those distinctive marks. It is not my intention to be offensive to others but only to locate, defend, and propagate Christ's true churches through the centuries. I realize that many will be offended, but it is my earnest prayer that they will overcome their distress and flee to Christ's church for refuge.

The Perpetuity of the Church

Matthew 16:18-19

One distinctive mark of Christ's church is Christ's promise of perpetuity. Jesus said, *"The gates of hell (Hades) shall not prevail against it."* Hell here is not the lake of fire and brimstone. "Hell" is better translated as Hades. Hades is the unseen realm of the dead. That is, His church would or could never be destroyed or annihilated. For sure, Christ built His church, instructed, and protected her while He was here. But the time came when Christ was to ascend back to the right hand of the Father. Before leaving earth he instructed His church that he would leave another comforter with her. John 14:16 *"And I will pray the Father, and he shall give you another Comforter, that he may abide with you for ever;"* John 14:26 *"But the Comforter, which is the Holy Ghost, whom the Father will send in my name, he shall teach you all things, and bring all things to your remembrance, whatsoever I have said unto you."* The Holy Spirit not only leads us unto all truths, but will also protect Christ's church until Christ comes in the eastern skies to receive her unto himself. This will be the first resurrection. We refer to this as the rapture of the saints.

Jesus also promised perpetuity in Matthew 28:18-20 ". . . . *lo, I am with you always, even unto the end of the world.*" (Age) We are now living near the end of this age and Christ is still with His church, and the church is still building up the Kingdom of God on earth. When this age draws to an end, Christ will return in the eastern skies and receive her unto himself, and she will forever be with the Lord.

The dark ages proved to be a very difficult time for the churches of Jesus Christ. Even though Christ promised her that annihilation would never happen, a time of tremendous persecution would reduce her number of being very many, down to very few and far in between. More details will be given to this in the next article.

Some churches such as the Mormon Church base their existence and foundation on the fact that Jesus either lied to his church or just wasn't able to protect her from annihilation. The Mormon Church (Latter Day Saints) claim that the church Jesus instituted during his life on earth really was completely and totally wiped off the face of the earth, and was later reinstituted by God through Joseph Smith. Thus they call themselves the Latter Day Saints. However, Jesus really did keep his promise and really did preserve his church. His church is still here doing his work. We have Christ's promise, and we believe it.

Perpetuating Churches

Much controversy has sprung up over the last hundred years or so, concerning the perpetuating of newly founded churches. Some churches cease to exist and new churches spring up in their place. Thus there is a continuous existence of true churches on earth at all times since Christ built the first church in Jerusalem.

E.M.D.A.

The question is how do these new churches perpetuate? Within the last century there arose a new theory teaching a chain-link, or E.M.D.A. (Essential Mother-Daughter Authority). This teaching claims that an already established church must grant authority to establish a new church before the new church could ever possibly become a properly organized church. The idea is that Jesus first gave the church at Jerusalem this authority, and then Jerusalem was to pass on this authority to form other churches (Matthew 28:18-20). Therefore all churches become a part of the church at Jerusalem. This authority has been (if true) passed down from one church to another church throughout the last two thousand years.

This theory over the last hundred or so years has become very popular among certain Baptist churches. Any church found not to have received this authority from another church was deemed an irregular and unscriptural church. One of the reasons this E.M.D.A. theory became so popular is because it was a very convenient measuring stick in determining the scriptualness of another church or churches. Convenience however, should never be a guide for truth. Scripture alone must be our guide.

How can a church begin as a mother-daughter relationship, and end up as a sister-sister relationship. That has a ring of inconsistency to it. They claim "like-begets-like". This is what God intended in creation. However, a church isn't created, nor is a church born of a church. Churches are built not born. All of this means the chain-link, E.M.D.A. doctrine is not founded in Holy writ. It is an invention of man.

There is also lacking any writings from our Baptist forefathers in our church history, prior to the twentieth century concerning any chain-link or E.M.D.A. This is a new doctrine thought up within the last hundred years or so, and we don't need any new doctrines.

Self-Constituting of Churches

Another theory is termed as the "self-constituting of churches". Matthew 28:18 says, *"All power (authority) is given unto me in heaven and in earth."* No-where in scripture are we told that Jesus transferred this authority to mere man, or to any church. We are completely devoid of any scriptural warrant concerning any E.M.D.A. teaching. Again I emphasis, the Bible is our final authority, in all matters of faith order and practice. If the Bible doesn't teach it, we shouldn't teach it. When the Bible is silent we should be silent.

Matthew 18:20 *"For where two or three are gathered together in my name, there am I in the midst of them."* The only authority needed to establish a new church comes directly from Jesus Christ. The real acid test of the scriptualness of a church lies in the distinguishing marks of a scriptural church. Does a church meet the pattern Jesus and the Apostles laid out in the New Testament?

Where two or three (or more) saved, and properly baptized saints covenant together and meet to establish a church by faith in Jesus Christ, is the beginning of a newly built church. This term is "self-constituting of churches". This seems to be the mode of founding and perpetuating churches in the New Testament.

It is true that the church at Jerusalem did aid the saints at Antioch in establishing them into a church. When the Jerusalem church heard of the new converts in Antioch, they had compassion on them and were eager to help them build a new church there. It's common for churches to co-operate with one another in the advancing the Kingdom of God on earth. Still every church remains independent of one another, and is under the sole rule of its head and founder Jesus Christ. Thus every church is always and only executive and never legislative.

The Persecution of the Church

The Holy scriptures make it very clear that we will be persecuted, and may even be put to death. Matthew 5 gives us an account of the Beatitudes. These Beatitudes should describe the life-style of those members of Christ's church. Jesus also describes the persecution that would follow the lives of his dedicated children. Matthew 5:10-12 *"Blessed are they which are persecuted for righteousness sake for theirs is the kingdom of heaven. (11) Blessed are ye, when men shall revile you, and persecute you, and shall say all manner of evil against you falsely, for my sake. (12) Rejoice, and be exceeding glad: for great is your reward in heaven: for so persecuted they the prophets which were before you."* If the prophets were persecuted, why shouldn't we also be persecuted? Consider also Christ's persecution and crucifixion. Matthew 10:24 *"The disciple is not above his master, nor the servant above his lord."* We are to be exceedingly glad and count it an honor to suffer for the cause of Christ.

It shouldn't be considered a strange thing for saints in Christ's church to be hated and mistreated. The fact of the matter is, if we're not persecuted we should be asking the question, why aren't we?

I fear the reason for the lack of persecution of Christ's churches today may lie in our lack of proclaiming the truth in today's world. Could it be we don't want to be offensive, so we withhold the truth? Consider Romans 1:18 *"For the wrath of God is revealed from heaven against all ungodliness and unrighteousness of men, who hold the truth in unrighteousness."* Are we more concerned with being offensive to man then proclaiming God's truth? May God help us!

The early churches weren't shy about guarding against false gospels entering into the churches. They were very aware of the warning Christ gave to his church through the Apostle Paul's writings. Galatians 1:6-12, and II Timothy 3:1-7; 13-17, and 4:2-5. The early churches were more concerned about keeping the church pure from apostasy then offending others or being persecuted themselves. And history records they were persecuted and martyred. Over fifty million saints were killed during twelve hundred years from the fifth century into the seventeenth century. Entire congregations were slaughtered, beheaded, burned at the stake, etc. All because they would not submit to infant baptism, baptizing by pouring or sprinkling, or joining the Church of Rome. Even though the early churches were many in number and scattered all around the countries of the world. They through the years became very few and far in-between. The Catholic Church and later the Protestants tried with everything they had to wipe Christ's churches off the face of the earth. Were it not for Christ's promise of perpetuity given to her by Christ himself she probably would have ceased to exist. I challenge you to read "Foxes Christian Martyrs of the World". In its pages describes real historical accounts of saints dying for the cause of Christ and his church. True life examples of what our Baptist forefathers endured in order to keep Christ's churches pure, and the gospel protected.

What really concerns me now is why the intensity of this persecution has stopped or at least lessened in the world today. Is it because the world is more civilized? NO! I fear much of it is because we have lessened in our preaching of the truth. Have we put our own welfare above the welfare of the gospel? It would seem so. It's not that I'm asking to be persecuted, just wondering why the church of today isn't. There must be a reason.

But to be sure, the persecution will again arise in the last days. Saints of God will go through a time of testing under the control of anti-Christ. This will be a time of great tribulation referred to in Matthew 24:21-22. Christ's church and many other saints will still be here to endure this time. Immediately following this the rapture of the saints will occur, and we will forever be with the Lord. Persecution is in our history as well as our future. Do we believe it, and are we ready for it?

Religious Liberty

It should be noted here about the importance of religious liberty. History proves that the Baptist churches during the Dark Ages were tremendously persecuted for the cause of Christ. Religious liberty was denied to them. Yet they have always granted religious liberty to others and have never persecuted anyone.

I take a strong stand in defending Christ's true church and always ready to expose error as scripture instructs. However, false churches have a right to exist, and I will never advocate persecuting them or trying to annihilate them as they have us.

Some of what they teach is true, and God will always bless his truth, whoever teaches it.

Separation of Church and State

Even though Baptists have been persecuted and martyred in the cruelest of ways. The Baptists have never persecuted others. Baptist history is recorded in a trail of blood beginning in the first century. One only has to read the Gospels and the Acts of the Apostles to learn of persecutions during the first century. John the Baptist, Stephen, and all the Apostles (except John) were killed. John was sent into exile to Patmos where he penned the Revelation of Jesus Christ.

Through the centuries the church of Jesus Christ grew amid the cruelest of persecution. As noted earlier, in the dark ages over fifty million Baptist were slain, be-headed, burn at the stake, buried alive, tortured, dismembered alive, yet they have never (according to history) persecuted anyone. Religious liberty was always taught and practiced through the years by the Baptists. In fact, it was the very first constitution written in America by a Baptist colony in Rhode Island that contained in its pages "Religious Liberty" in the year of 1663. This came about by the efforts of Roger Williams and John Clark. While still under England's rule, and after twelve patient years, John Clark finally received approval from England to establish a Baptist colony with a constitution of its own. It was then that religious liberty first became the law of the land.

The Baptists were also the chief instruments in completing the constitution of the United States, the charter of revolutionary liberty, by adding the amendment securing full religious freedom. The first amendment to the United States constitution was added in 1789. It reads, "Congress shall make no law respecting an establishment of religion, or prohibiting the free exercise thereof, or abridging the freedom of speech, or of the press, or the rights of the people peaceably to assemble and to petition the government for a redress of grievances."

America has never known any greater patriots than our Baptist forefathers, the very ones who have been martyred and cruelly persecuted. The very Baptists that have been hated through the years are the very ones who have secured religious liberty for all others. Every person should have the right to worship according to the dictates of their own conscience.

The Nature of the Church

Matthew 16:18

The type of church Jesus built is also of enormous importance. Jesus built a local and visible church. Jesus said, "I will build my 'Ekklesia' church". Jesus used the Greek word "Ekklesia", which translated to English is a congregation or an assembly. Either congregation or assembly must be understood as a visible gathering of people in one location at any one time. Thus Christ's church is a church meeting together in one place at any given time. Again any honest exegetical interpretation of scripture will disprove and expose any idea of a universal or invisible church as false, and any church teaching such is a false church.

It is also not to be underestimated the importance of the material Jesus used to build His Ekklesia (church). Members of the church Jesus built are a regenerated people who were baptized by John the Baptist. Luke 1:17b *"to make ready a people prepared for the Lord."* John came preaching in the wilderness to make disciples, which he then baptized for Jesus to build His church with. John would not baptize those who were not saved, and those not saved or baptized could not be members of the church Jesus built. Notice John came to make ready an already saved people and prepare them by baptizing them. These saved and baptized people Jesus used as material to build His church.

Again being honest with scripture, we must conclude the church Jesus built is an assembly of regenerated believers and baptized by immersion before becoming material for Jesus to use to build His church. Anything short of this is not a scriptural church.

I Cor. 12:28a, *"And God hath set some in the church, first apostles,"* The first members Christ used as building material were the apostles. Matthew 4:18-22 Peter, Andrew, James, and John were the first members of Christ's church. Those saved, and baptized by John (later called the Baptist). Here we see the first forming of a local and visible church that Jesus built. Nothing short of this will ever suffice.

Autonomy of the Church

The first church was located at Jerusalem. It was a local assemble of saints baptized by John the Baptist. It grew rapidly in and around Jerusalem but had at first a very limited commission. Luke 24:47-49 *"And that repentance and remission of sins should be preached in his name among all nations, beginning at Jerusalem. (48) And ye are witnesses of these things. (49) And, behold, I send the promise of my Father upon you: but tarry ye in the city of Jerusalem until ye be endued with power from on high."* Jesus' church would ultimately receive a worldwide commission but not until she was "endued with power from on high." Acts 1:8 *"But ye shall receive power, after that the Holy Ghost is come upon you: and ye shall be witnesses unto me both in Jerusalem, and in all Judaea, and in Samaria, and unto the uttermost part of the earth."* Jesus instituted His church Himself and none other. It was during His earthly ministry. However, she was granted at that time a very limited commission. It wasn't until fifty days after Christ's crucifixion that His church received a worldwide commission. It was the day of Pentecost, fifty days after Christ's crucifixion that she was endued with power from on high. Acts 2:1 *"And when the day of*

Pentecost was fully come, they were all with one accord in one place."
The church at Jerusalem was a local, and visible church located at one
location at one time. Fifty days after Christ's crucifixion. The church
was already in existence and operating under a limited commission,
and awaiting the day she would be endued with power from on high.
That day has come. It was the day of Pentecost, and she (Christ's
church) was to be baptized by the Holy Spirit. Acts 2:22 *"And suddenly
there came a sound from heaven as of a rushing mighty wind, and it
filled all the house where they were sitting."* The entire room was filled
with the Holy Spirit. Hence they were immersed in the Holy Spirit, or
baptized in the Holy Spirit. This was a onetime event that the church
was baptized by the Holy Spirit. The same church of Jerusalem that
was baptized by the Holy Spirit has now expanded into many churches
around the world. Every scriptural church today was represented by the
one Jerusalem church. She is the same church but has many different
localities and different names. That one baptism of the Holy Spirit was
for all time, and all true churches.

Many claim the day of Pentecost is the birth of the church;
however this idea is very wrong. The church truly was empowered on
that day, but she existed many days or possibly years before. I don't
mean to diminish the importance of that day, but it wasn't the birth
of the church. Christ later gave her a worldwide commission. Matthew
28:18-20

Getting back to the autonomy of the church; we should notice
especially in the Acts of the Apostles that every church acted within
its own capacity. No one church acted over or expressed authority
over another church. There existed no hierarchy or denominational
headquarters to rule over any church or churches. Every church had its
own church membership roll. The church at Jerusalem before Pentecost
had a membership of an hundred and twenty. Acts 1:15 they had a
business meeting to elect an Apostle to replace Judas. Acts 1:21-26. The
church had to choose between Joseph and Matthias. The church voted
to receive Matthias as a replacement of Judas.

Church polity is an important distinctive mark in Christ's church. After being led by the Holy Spirit, the church at Antioch voted to release Barnabas and Saul to be missionaries. Acts 13:1-6. The early churches exercised a pure democracy type of government. The majority ruled the actions and activities of the church. Every member had a vote.

The apostles alone had leadership over the churches only during the infancy of the churches as they then needed extra guidance. The office of apostleship was finished as the churches matured. Even pastor's, though they are leaders of the church are not to rule over God's heritage but as examples to the flock. I Peter 5:1-3

Jesus Christ is the only head of the church. Ephesians 5:23b *"Christ is the head of the church: and he is the saviour of the body."* and Colossians 1:18 *"And he is the head of the body, the church who is the beginning, the firstborn from the dead; that in all things he might have the preeminence."*

The churches' only "walking orders" is the Bible. We are bound by and to it. Everything taught in our churches needs to be a "thus saith the Lord." If it cannot be proven in the Bible it ought not to be taught in the church. Yet every act of any church has only Christ to answer to and not a denomination, hierarchy, or presbytery of men. No government of men can dictate to us or us to them.

We render unto Caesar the things that are Caesar's and unto God the things that are God's. Matthew 22:21.

The following is a quote from the late Dr. Norman H. Wells from his article "Every Bible-Believing Baptist Should Belong to an Independent Baptist Church"

An Independent Baptist Church

An independent Baptist Church believes that the only organization given in the New Testament is the local church. They believe that God has given the church as the means of accomplishing His purpose in this age.

An independent Baptist Church, therefore, does not affiliate or identify themselves with any organized Convention, Association or Fellowship.

An independent Baptist Church sends forth its missionaries by the authority of the church and not through an unscriptural Mission Board. These missionaries are supported directly by the churches.

An independent Baptist Church cooperates with other Baptist Churches in missions, schools, etc. but does so on a voluntary basis and without any unscriptural organization binding the churches together.

An independent Baptist Church refuses to compromise the historical Baptist doctrines for the sake of popular appeal.

An independent Baptist Church has to rely upon God and give Him all the glory.

True Baptists love the church that Jesus loved and will not have this love and loyalty switched to some man-made organization.

An independent Baptist Church is not dictated to nor influenced by any head or headquarters except Jesus Christ.

The Ordinances of the Church

Jesus put two ordinances in his church, these being baptism and the Lord's Supper. These two are the very heart of the church, and need to be taken very seriously. Paul gives the church at Corinth very stringent orders I Corinthians 11:2b *"keep the ordinances, as I delivered them to you.*" These two ordinances will go far as distinguishing marks of a scriptural church. Get these two ordinances wrong and the whole church is wrong and unscriptural. Everything that the church is instructed to do is clearly told how to do them. Anything a church may do that is not instructed to do, or is not instructed how to do it, shouldn't do it. This certainly includes all Babylonian holidays (Easter, Valentines, Halloween, lent, Christmas, etc.) These are inventions of sinful corrupt man, and not found in scripture. These ordinances will make or break a church and will go far in determining its scriptualness with Christ.

Baptism

John the Baptist was sent by God, Luke 1:17c "*to make ready a people prepared for the Lord.*" The READY people are a saved people. John took those saved saints and baptized them to make them PREPARED for the Lord to build His church with. These saved and baptized saints are the materials Christ needed to build His church. Matthew 3:1-8 John the Baptist was preparing the material Christ was to build his church with by baptizing them.

Notice first, John's refusal to baptize many, calling them vipers. These showed no evidence of conversion Matthew 3:8 "*Bring forth therefore fruits meet for repentance;*" Without a profession of faith and evidence of repentance John knew their salvation was not authentic. The only fit subject for baptism is true conversion. Notice secondly, Acts 8:26-40. Philip preached Christ to an Ethiopian eunuch, and he was saved. As they journeyed along they came to water and the eunuch asked to be baptized. Philip answered, "*If thou believest with all thine heart thou mayest and he answered and said, I believe that Jesus is the Son of God.*" They went into the water and Philip baptized the eunuch.

Acts 16:19-33, Paul and Silas were imprisoned for preaching the gospel. During the night an earthquake opened all the prison doors and released the prisoners. The prison guard feared for his life and was ready to kill himself, but Paul cautioned him. He then fell at Paul's feet and trembling asked Paul, "*What must I do to be saved? And they said Believe on the Lord Jesus Christ, and thou shalt be saved. And he took them the same hour of the night and washed their stripes, and was baptized."* Baptism is always to follow conversion. Any baptism preceding conversion is a complete waste of time and energy. On the day of Pentecost those that gladly received his word were baptized. Acts 2:41 Peter was preaching to some Gentiles in Acts 10:44-48. Peter said, *"Can any man forbid water, that these should not be baptize, which have received the Holy Ghost as well as we? And he commanded them to be baptized in the name of the Lord."* Many other scriptures can be found that prove baptism is only by complete submersion in water of a newly converted child of God. A saved (by God's grace) person is an only fit subject for baptism.

The mode of baptism is also very important. "Baptize" is a transliteration of the Greek word "baptizo", which means to bury, plunge, or dip. Baptizing is a picture of Christ's death, burial, and resurrection. Romans 6:3-10 is a wonderful description of our being baptized (buried) with Christ to show his death, burial, and resurrection. No sprinkling or pouring could ever show this. Remember Paul admonishes us *"to keep the ordinances as I have delivered them to you."* I Cor. 11:2

I cannot emphasis strong enough or often enough the importance of this ordinance to keep it pure and unchanged.

Lord's Supper

This ordinance was given by Christ to commemorate his death, burial and resurrection till he returns. I Corinthians 11:24-26. The Lord's Supper is a memorial meal to be observed until he comes to receive his church unto himself at the rapture. *"This do in remembrance of me."*

The unleavened bread is to commemorate his broken (crucified) body, and the cup is to commemorate his shed blood he shed for his elect.

Only unleavened bread can represent his sinless body broken for the sins of His people. Only wine (pure red wine without added leavening) can represent Christ's sinless and shed blood, shed for his elect. No substitutes or alterations can be accepted. This is a very solemn observance and not to be taken lightly or with unconfessed sins.

Neither of these ordinances are requirements to salvation. Salvation is by grace through faith Ephesians 2:8-9. These must only follow salvation. They are evidences of salvation not the cause of salvation.

Closed Communion

The Lord's Supper is a closed celebration; closed to the membership of a particular church. That is, this ordinance is closed to all but its own members. Every body of believers, scripturally baptized is to participate together with its own membership.

Every local body is independent of all other bodies. Thus, every church is a custodian of the Lord's Table, and therefore is to protect it by strict rules given to it by its head, Jesus Christ. We have no right to invite anyone to it from any other body of Christ, as we remain independent from them.

The Offices of the Church

Christ placed two offices in his church, these being the Bishop or Elder (Pastor) and deacons. Both of these have requirements set in scripture and must be closely followed. Both are to be filled only by the men of the church according to the scriptural requirements.

Pastor

The Pastors are to feed the flock of God which God hath set them over. I Peter 5:2-3 *"Feed the flock of God which is among you, taking the oversight thereof, not by constraint, but willingly, not for filthy lucre, but of a ready mind: (3) Neither as being lords over God's heritage, but being examples to the flock."* II Timothy 4:2, 5 *"Preach the word; be instant in season, out of season; reprove, rebuke, exhort with all longsuffering and doctrine. (5) But watch thou in all things, endure afflictions, do the work of an evangelist, make full proof of thy ministry."* It is not his position to tickle the ears of the flock, but rather rebuke, exhort, and reprove when necessary. His requirements are set forth in I Timothy 3:1-7, and Titus 1:6-9. Among those are of good reputation, husband of one wife, vigilant, sober, of good behavior, given to hospitality, able to teach, non-alcoholic drinker, not greedy, patient and peace loving, and one who rules his own house well. Must be a matured Christian with experience, and able to lead. He must rightly divide (interpret) the word of God. II Timothy 2:15.

He needs to be upheld by the flock with much prayer, encouragement and support. His, is not a popularity position but a God given position. He is to lead and not herd the flock of God.

Deacons

The need for deacons springs from a problem arising from within the church. Physical needs arose requiring someone to oversee these physical needs. Acts 6:1-3 (3) *"Wherefore, brethren, look ye out among you seven men of honest report, full of the Holy Ghost and wisdom, whom we may appoint over this business."*

The requirements of deacons are also laid out in scripture. I Timothy 3:8-13. Not double tongued, not given to much wine, not greedy of filthy lucre; earnest, have demonstrated themselves worthy, have one faithful Christian wife, not slanderers, loyal in all things and have ruled well in their own homes. Not all can meet these requirements.

Both offices

All actions of the church are to be filled by the men of the church. This is very clear in scripture. Acts 6:3 *"look ye out among you seven*

MEN". I Timothy 3:2 "HUSBAND of one wife" and (12) "HUSBAND of one wife."

The ladies of the church are to be in silence and in subjection to the men. This is not to say they are any less in character or inferior to the men. Theirs is also not to teach or lead the congregation in public prayer. I Timothy 2:11-12 "Let the woman learn in silence with all subjection. (12) *But I suffer not a woman to teach, nor to usurp authority over the man, but to be in silence.*" I Thessalonians 5:25 and II Thessalonians 3:1 "*BRETHREN, pray for us*" Also, I Timothy 2:8a. "*I will therefore that men pray every where,*" No this is not me saying this, nor is it the Koran. It is God speaking to us in His holy word, the Bible. It's not up to us to agree or disagree. Whenever we disagree with God, we are always wrong and He is always right. The Bible is our final rule in all matters of faith, order, and practice.

The Discipline of the Church

"*Moreover if thy brother shall trespass against thee, go and tell him his fault between thee and him alone: if he shall hear thee, thou hast gained thy brother. (16) But if he will not hear thee, then take with thee one or two more, that in the mouth of two or three witnesses every word may be established. (17) And if he shall neglect to hear them, tell it unto the church: but if he neglect to hear the church, let him be unto thee as an heathen man and a publican.*" Matthew 18:15-17. Here is another aspect of the church which is sadly neglected, yet clearly taught in scripture. His church is to be a pure church, a blameless church, a chaste church. II Corinthians 11:2 "*For I am jealous over you with godly jealousy: for I have espoused you to one husband that I may present you as a chaste virgin to Christ.*" Understand, as long as His church remains on earth and run by mere men she will not be perfect. That will come after she is raptured and present with Christ. However, here on earth she is to be as pure as humanly possible. She consists of saved and baptized members. Who are living as pure and Holy lives as possible. She must strive to have the mind of Christ, and remove sin from within. Much like a ship in the sea, a ship can thrive in a body of water so long as the water remains outside. A church can survive in a world of sin so long as the sin remains outside her membership. A church that abides in sin is like a ship filled with water. It will fail. I Corinthians 5:1-13. The early church was a church of new born again babes in Christ who thought they were doing the right thing by overlooking and tolerating the sins of some of its members. I Corinthians 5:1. One who was having an affair with his step-mother? Paul clearly instructed them to exclude such an one from among them, and to stand ready to judge among their own members. Matthew 18:16-18 says if a brother offends you, you should go to him and seek to work it out privately. If it can be worked out, all is well. If not take another two or three brethren with you that all can be established. Hopefully the problem can then be corrected. But if he continues the offense take it before the church, and if he still persists he is to be treated as and unsaved one and removed from the church role.

This has a dual purpose. First it is to purify the church of his or her sin, but also and just as important it is to teach the sinning one the error of their way, and hopefully cause them to repent and return to the church as a restored and honored member. The church is then privileged and obligated to forgive and restore him or her. II Corinthians 2:7 "... *ye ought rather to forgive him, and comfort him, lest perhaps such a one should be swallowed up with overmuch sorrow.*" Seldom will a church need to exercise all these steps. More times than not, someone in sin will be corrected with the first or second step. The church will be blessed and Christ will be pleased.

The Truthfulness of the Church

The true churches of Jesus Christ are distinguished by their conviction regarding the sufficiency and authority of the word of God. The Bible alone is the final authority in all matters of faith, order, and practice. The Old and New Testaments are God breathed, and stands infallible and without error in all of its parts. "*All scripture is given by inspiration of God, and is profitable for doctrine, for reproof, for correction, for instruction in righteousness: (17) That the man of God may be perfect (matured), thoroughly furnished unto all good works."* II Timothy 3:16-17. (Emphasis mine L.D.)

There is no institution in the world that contains more truth than the church Jesus built. It remains the pillar and ground of the truth. I Timothy 3:15 The Holy Spirit guides us unto all truths. There is nothing in this world more valued then the truth of God's word.

Christ's church is also distinguished by the doctrines of grace. That form of theology that embraces the total depravity of man, unconditional election, limited atonement, irresistible grace, and the perseverance and preservation of the saints. The fact that these are so hated in so-called Christian communities has no effect on their truthfulness or our willingness to proclaim them.

Modern Christendom only embraces that which man can control, and likes to believe. The doctrine of grace as taught in scripture, magnifies God, and humbles man. Just the opposite of what men seek. God's truth becomes secondary in today's Christendom. It seems man's own pleasure is merely and only what matters. II Timothy 3:1-7 *"This know also, that in the last days perilous times shall come. (2) For men shall be lovers of their own selves, covetous, boasters, proud, blasphemers, disobedient to parents, unthankful, unholy, (3) Without natural affection, trucebreakers, false accusers, incontinent, fierce, despisers of those that are good, (4) Traitors, heady highminded, lovers of pleasures more than lovers of God; (5) Having a form of godliness, but denying the power thereof; from such turn away. (6) For of this sort are they which creep into houses, and lead captive silly women laden with sins, led away with divers lusts, (7) Every learning, and never able to come to the knowledge of the truth."*

Sadly, God's truth is not primary in today's Christendom. Many times truth is set aside for the pleasures of sinful men. What is pleasing to the flesh overrides truth that doesn't appease the flesh.

Through the years the true churches have been blessed to have had men of valor. Men like John Bunyan, John Newton, Matthew Henry, Jonathan Edwards, Ben Bogard, J.R. Graves, J.M. Pendleton, J.P. Boyce, Charles Spurgeon, Arthur Pink, and a host of others that have not bowed to the pressures of apostasy, men of renown that preached the truth at any and all cost to themselves. We must understand however that we hold to these truths not because of these great saints before us, but because Jesus and the Apostles so clearly taught them. Our doctrines are not new doctrines; they're over six thousand years old. These go all the way back to Adam in the garden.

We receive truth from God and His word because we value truth. It is our heart beat, our reason for living. It is everything to us and we will claim it at all costs. But there must be a deep abiding desire from within your heart or the truth will escape you. *"Study to show thyself approved unto God, a workman that needeth not to be ashamed, rightly dividing the word of truth."* II Timothy 2:15. Much study is hard work, but the dividends paid are eternal.

The Purity of the Church

Another distinguishing mark of a scriptural church is the stand she takes against heresy and apostasy. Her members are to live holy lives, and that includes fleeing from all forms of idolatry. Truth must be defended and that many times means exposing heresy in all its forms. We are not to partake of the world and all its enticements. Scripture says, I John 2:15-17. *"Love not the world, neither the things that are in the world. If any man love the world, the love of the Father is not in him. (16) For all that is in the world, the lust of the flesh, and the lust of the eyes, and the pride of life, is not of the Father, but is of the world. (17) And the world passeth away, and the lust thereof: but he that doeth the will of God abideth for ever."* We are in the world but not of the world.

Living Holy lives is critical in the life of a Christian. Consider what Paul said in Hebrews 12:14 *"Follow peace with all men, and holiness, without which no man shall see the Lord:"* and II Corinthians 7:1

"*. . . . let us cleanse ourselves from all filthiness of the flesh and spirit, perfecting holiness in the fear of God.*" Our greatest enemies lie from within us. I John 2:16. "*For all that is in the world, the lust of the flesh, and the lust of the eyes, and the pride of life, is not of the Father, but is of the world.*"

Examples such as all the holidays of Babylon must be excluded from within the church, holidays like Valentine's Day, Easter, Halloween, Lent and Christmas. All of these came from Babylon, and were the reason God destroyed Babel and confounded their language before scattering them around the world. These were holidays Babylon used to worship false gods. These ceremonies became so ingrained in their lives that when God sent them around the world they took these traditions with them. But these traditions were all evil and idolatrous in nature.

The newly formed Catholic Church rescued these traditions and incorporated them into the Catholic Church. They just changed the names and added Christ birth and worship to them and passed them off as being Christian. In truth they are evil pagan holidays which angered God at Babylon. I invite you to investigate the true origin of Christmas, Valentines, Easter, and Halloween. Everything originating in or from Babylon should be exposed as satanic and avoided by Christians. Even steeples on church buildings come from Babylon and should be avoided.

II Corinthians 6:16-18 "*And what agreement hath the temple of God with idols? for ye are the temple of the living God; as God hath said, I will dwell in them, and walk in them; and I will be their God, and they shall be my people. (17) Wherefore come out from among them, and be ye separate, saith the Lord, and touch not the unclean thing; and I will receive you, (18) And will be a Father unto you, and ye shall be my sons and daughters, saith the Lord Almighty.*" The Catholic and Protestant churches have wrapped these celebrations up in a neat little package and passed them off as glorifying to God, but in reality are nothing but dead man's bones full of extortion and sin. I implore you to read the book, "The Two Babylon's" by Alexander Hislop. The Papal worship is proved to be the worship of Nimrod and his wife (Astarte). Nimrod was the builder of Babylon. Genesis 11:1-9.

The early church did not worship these forbidden holidays, and neither should we. It's interesting to note that in the early days of America during the time of the Puritans these Babylonian holidays were considered as evil pagan holidays and were outlawed in America.

The Glorious Church

Christ's churches have a wonderful and tremendously glorious future. She is espoused to Christ as a chaste virgin. II Corinthians 11:2 *"For I am jealous over you with godly jealousy for I have espoused you to one husband, that I may present you as a chaste virgin to Christ."*

One day Christ will appear in the eastern sky and receive his church along with many other redeemed and take them to glory. There will be the marriage supper of the lamb. Revelation 19:7-9 *"Let us be glad and rejoice, and give honour to him: for the marriage of the Lamb is come, and his wife had made herself ready. (8) And to her was granted that she should be arrayed in fine linen, clean and white: for the fine linen is the righteousness of the saints. (9) And he saith unto me, Write, Blessed are they which are called unto the marriage supper of the Lamb. And he saith unto me, These are the true sayings of God."*

Those who are the espoused to Christ are those faithful members of the church that Jesus built. Notice I said faithful members. Those who have become members but not faithful or those saved but not scripturally baptized or who have never been members of His church will be the guests at the marriage supper and the marriage ceremony. Also those espoused to Christ will enjoy a special place in heaven. Revelation 21:2 *"And I John saw the holy city, new Jerusalem, coming down from God out of heaven, prepared as a bride adorned for her husband."* Revelation 21:9-27 is a must read. Described is the New Jerusalem, a dwelling place for the bride of Christ. I picture this as coming down out of heaven and being suspended in air somewhat above the earth. More glorious then anything I could imagine or describe.

John the Baptist wasn't even a part of Christ bride or his church. John 3:29. John was a friend of the bridegroom, but not the bride. Yet in this he was pleased.

The Old Testament saints were not espoused to Christ as there was not an Old Testament church. The church Jesus built is a New Testament institution.

Summary

There are many false churches which meet some of the distinguishing marks of the church Jesus built. However, there remains only one true church that has existed in every century from Christ to the present day that can meet all the distinguishing marks of Christ's church. These are called Baptist churches.

It is also true that many irregular Baptist churches have used and miss-used the Baptist name, and have tarnished it over centuries. Yet Christ's churches still remain on earth, and are still carrying on the work Christ commissioned her to do.

It is up to each of us to search out the scriptures and identify that church. Her distinguishing marks are recorded in the New Testament. Mainly found in the Acts of the Apostles and the Gospels of Christ.

It is my prayer, and greatest heart's desire that there will be many that will read this, and be inspired to search out and find the only church that Jesus is head and founder of. Only in this church will Christ ever be glorified. Ephesians 3:21 *"Unto him be glory in the church by Jesus Christ throughout all ages, world without end. Amen."*

CHAPTER 12
Personal Seperation

W e, being God's elect are admonished in God's word to have no fellowship with this present world, but rather reprove them.

Ephesians 5:11-12, *"And have no fellowship with the unfruitful works of darkness, but rather reprove them. (12) For it is a shame even to speak of those things which are done of them in secret."*

John 15:18-19, *"If the world hate you, ye know that it hated me before it hated you. (19) If ye were of the world, the world would love its own; but because ye are not of the world, but I have chosen you out of the world, therefore the world hateth you."*

John 16:33, *"These things I have spoken unto you, that ye might have peace. In the world ye shall have tribulation: but be of good cheer; I have overcome the world."*

I've learned very early in my Christian walk of the truth of God's word. This world has no time or desire to know of God, his word or his people.

John 17:14-16, *"I have given them thy word, and the world hath hated them, because they are not of the world, even as I am not of the world. (15) I pray not that thou shouldest take them out of the world, but that thou shouldest keep them from the evil. (16) They are not of the world, even as I am not of the world."*

We are in the world, but not of the world. Here in this world we must abide, and serve, but our hearts are far from here. Our spirits are with Christ, and He with us. The Holy Spirit has taken residence within us, and will guide us unto all truths. We as God's elect have an unquenchable thirst to know more of Christ, and His word. We have an overwhelming desire to serve, and please Him.

We as God's elect are also longing to meet the Lord in the air, that where He is we may be also. We with great anticipation are longing for that day referred to as our blessed hope.

Titus 2:13 *"Looking for that blessed hope, and the glorious appearing of the great God and our Saviour Jesus Christ."*

I Thessalonians 4:13-17 *"But I would not have you to be ignorant, brethren, concerning them which are asleep, (have died) that ye sorrow not, even as others which have no hope. (14) For if we believe that Jesus died and rose again, even so them also which sleep in Jesus will God bring with him. (15) For this we say unto you by the word of the Lord, that we which are alive and remain unto the coming of the Lord shall not prevent [precede] them which are asleep. (16) For the Lord himself shall descend from heaven with a shout, with the voice of an archangel, and with the trump of God: and the dead in Christ shall rise first: (17) Then we which are alive and remain shall be caught up together with them in the clouds, to meet the Lord in the air: and so shall we ever be with the Lord."* [Emphasis mine L.D.] II Timothy 4:8, *"Henceforth there is laid for me a crown of righteousness, which the Lord, the righteous judge, shall give me at that day: and not to me only, but unto all them also that LOVE HIS APPEARING."* ([Emphasis mine, L.D.)

I must repeat the words of John the revelator in Revelations 22:20 *"Even so, come, Lord Jesus."*

I have little or no problem leaving this world behind. There is a better world ahead. Today I'm imprisoned in this body, and on this world. The day is coming when I'll scale the utmost heights, and live eternally. I will be free to live with the one who died for me. But, my days of service here below have not ended. So what's my course?

Ephesians 5:15-20, *"See then that ye walk circumspectly, not as fools, but as wise, (16) Redeeming the time, because the days are evil. (17) Wherefore be ye not unwise, but understanding what the will of the Lord is. (18) And be not drunk with wine, wherein is excess; but be filled with the Spirit. (19) Speaking to yourself in psalms and hymns and spiritual songs, singing and making melody in your heart to the Lord; (20) Giving thanks always for all things unto God and the Father in the name of our Lord Jesus Christ;"*

Walking circumspectly is walking cautiously, and understanding that the days we live in are evil days. Knowing what the will of God is for our lives, avoiding the appearance of evil, and encouraging and strengthening ourselves with the knowledge of God, and His word. Oh, the strength that can be had in singing hymns and spiritual songs, and making melody in our hearts.

Fellowship can be very important providing we fellowship with those who know, or at least desire to know more of God's word. But avoid fellowshipping with the world or worldly people. Nonbelievers, or as the scriptures put it "the natural man" knows nothing of God or his word, and should be witnessed to, but short on fellowshipping with. Their eyes are blinded by the god of this world, and have no desire or ability to understand or come to Christ for salvation. This is a work that can only be accomplished by a triune God.

I Corinthians 2:14 *"But the natural man receiveth not the things of the spirit of God: for they are foolishness unto him: neither can he know them, because they are spiritually discerned."*

Our only message to them should be their sinfulness, and their need of a savior which is Christ the Lord.

I have very dear loved ones who have never tasted that the Lord is gracious, and I full well understand that they may never be saved. This knowledge at times is more than I can contain. God is a just and righteous God, and they are in His hands. I understand their plight may be eternal condemnation, and utter helplessness, and hopelessness. Should they leave this world in their present state, hell will be their home throughout endless ages. Perhaps, because of this I have been a little overbearing with the gospel message.

They have rejected both Christ and the gospel message. Losing them to the forces of Satan will be just, simply because of their own rejection of Christ. It will be just on God's part, but painful on my part.

The bottom line is God is a just and righteous God to all of humanity, but forgiving only those with the faith of and from Christ. It's not our faith in Christ but Christ's faith in us, and toward Him.

New Converts

I'm both sad and perplexed concerning new converts that remain satisfied with the milk of the word, and remain as babes in Christ.

Hebrews 5:11-14, "*Of whom we have many things to say, and hard to be uttered, seeing ye are dull of hearing. (12) For when for the time ye ought to be teachers, ye have need that one teach you again which be the first principles of the oracles of God; and are become such as have need of milk, and not of strong meat. (13) For every one that useth milk is unskillful in the word of righteousness: for he is a babe. (14) But strong meat belongeth to them that are of full age, even those who by reason of use have their senses exercised to discern both good and evil.*"

Those who have been born again, yet with one hand behind their backs hanging on to the world, and the worldly system will have great difficulty discerning God's word, and God's will for their lives. These are they that will spend all their lives on being bottle feed.

Also these may abide in a counterfeit church that feeds nothing but the bottle to their members. Such is the case with Catholic and protestant churches. However, it's not just these, but many other churches that seek to please and tickle the ears of the hearers. Preachers can preach for hours without ever getting into the meat of the word. These people come to the service not expecting to learn anything because they've never learned anything before. These have become so dormant in their Christian lives that when they do hear some great truth they reject it as false.

These have become comatose, and are rendered useless. This is proof positive that we are saved by the grace of God.

There should be a thirsting after the knowledge of God and His word, and a strong and healthy desire to know more, more about Jesus and His word.

Elisa Hewitt in her hymn says it this way:

> More about Jesus would I know, more of his grace to others show;
> More of his saving fullness see, More of his love who died for me.
> More about Jesus let me learn, more of his holy will discern;
> Spirit of God, my teacher be, showing the things of God to me.
> More about Jesus in his word, Holding communion with my Lord;
> Hearing his voice in every line, Making each faithful saying mine.
> More about Jesus on his throne, Riches in glory all his own;
> More of his Kingdom's sure increase, More
> of his coming, Prince of Peace.

Occasionally, we may find those who make a good profession of faith, and at times show some shallow fruits of salvation. Yet after years of growth they show little or no maturity. This is indeed troubling and sad, and causes us to wonder about the genuineness of their salvation. We must leave them in the hands of our Savior.

II Thessalonians 2:13 "... *God hath from the beginning chosen you to salvation through sanctification of the Spirit and belief of the truth:*"

I understand the uniqueness of every person, and I also understand the measure of faith given to all God's elect differs. We all have a different calling. Still I have much trouble believing that God is pleased with a saint who is nourished from the bottle year after year.

Romans 12:3, *"For I say, through the grace given unto me, to every man that is among you, not to think of himself more highly than he ought to think; but to think soberly, according as God hath dealt to every man the measure of faith."*

Every child of God needs some maturing (sanctification) and a belief of God's truth or his salvation is flowed and his profession of faith is hallow.

I, for one have and continue to have trouble in this area. I thought all saints should see and understand what I see and understand. I would like to be another Charles Spurgeon, but that's not my calling. If God reveals a certain truth to me I immediately want to share it with the world, and wonder why the world doesn't want to know about it. This very well may be a problem I'll take to the grave. I guess realizing the problem is the first step to overcoming it. Also I'm certain that along the way I've offended some I shouldn't have, and others I haven't offended that I should have. Perhaps that makes me human and vulnerable to error.

Then there are those who refuse the strong meat, and insist on being bottle feed. They resist the truth and are not teachable. What are we to do with these?

II Thessalonians 3:6 *"Now we command you, brethren, in the name of our Lord Jesus Christ, that ye withdraw yourself from every BROTHER that walketh disorderly, and not after the tradition which ye received of us."* (Emphasis mine L.D.)

Titus 3:9-11, *"But avoid foolish questions, and genealogies, and contentions, and strivings about the law; for they are unprofitable and vain. (10) A man that is an heretic after the first and second admonition reject; (11) Knowing that he that is such is subverted, and sinneth, being condemned of himself."*

This can be heartbreaking and discouraging. Yet we are admonished by Holy writ, and compelled to do so. This isn't fun, nor is it easy. However, as with all of God's commands, it is proper and correct to do so.

As already stated, we have a responsibility to walk circumspectly, orderly, soberly, and avoid the very appearance of evil. That must also mean to withdraw and have no fellowship from all enticements of this world. This makes our relationship with Christ a personal relationship. This is for nonbelievers and some believers as well.

II Corinthians 6:14-18 *"Be ye not unequally yoked together with unbelievers: for what fellowship hath righteousness with unrighteousness? and what communion hath light with darkness? (15) And what concord hath Christ with Belial? or what part hath he that believeth with an infidel? (16) And what agreement hath the temple of God with idols? for ye are the temple of the living God; as God hath said, I will dwell in them, and walk in them; and I will be their God, and they shall be my people. (17) Wherefore come out from among them, and be ye separate, saith the Lord, and touch not the unclean thing; and I will receive you, (18) And will be a Father unto you, and ye shall be my sons and daughters, saith the Lord Almighty."*

Our walk with Christ must be a personal, orderly and obedient journey that is pleasing to Christ. Always understand that the Holy Scriptures are the final authority in all matters of faith, order, and practice. The King James Version of the Bible is our walking orders, and the only version to be trusted.

Being unequally yoked together with unbelievers includes all kinds of ventures such as pleasure, business, and marital unions. Marriage is of one husband, one wife, during one lifetime. This union becomes a home, which is the first institution God placed on earth, and is the bond of this earth. It sickens me to see a broken home. Yet the scriptures couldn't be clearer. Over half of the homes in America have and are being broken. There is so little thought given to the sanctity of marriage and the precious gifts that God has given to us. It's a popular thing today to be divorced. There is a popular TV show for our young people to watch called, "Happily Divorced". Today being divorced is the in thing, the thing to do. Pride is taken in announcing their divorce. *"Even so, Lord Jesus, come quickly."* If believers can't fellowship with nonbelievers how can they then unite in marriage? This marriage is a disaster in the making. It's not God's way. Broken hearts, broken homes, sadness and sorrow are sure to follow.

We must survive in this world while we're here, but survival doesn't mean enjoying it and becoming a part of it. We must rub elbows with those around us at the work place, the mall, the grocery store, etc. Tell them the good news of the gospel, be kind, loving and friendly yet withdraw from openly fellowshipping with them.

If I'm walking down a street with a nonbeliever I should be telling him about Jesus dying for sinners, but if he suddenly turns into a tavern, I'll not follow him there. I will shake the dirt off my feet and walk away. In short you cannot have a personal relationship with the world and with Christ at the same time.

Matthew 6:24 *"No man can serve two masters: for either he will hate the one, and love the other, or else he will hold to the one, and despise the other. Ye cannot serve God and mammon."*

CHAPTER 13

A Look at the Order of Subordination

In the Home

There is much controversy over the scriptural teachings of this important subject. There is perhaps no other subject more sensitive to the ladies of the church, and understandably so. While the world is calling for complete equality in all matters, the saints of God know this is not only impossible, but also impractical, and unbiblical.

Will you join with me as we prayerfully, and earnestly search the scriptures to find the mind of Christ in this matter?

According to the apostle Paul, the wife is to be subordinate to her husband.

Ephesians 5:22-33 *"Wives, submit yourselves unto your own husbands, as unto the Lord. (23) For the husband is the head of the wife, even as Christ is the head of the church: and he is the savior of the body. (24) Therefore as the church is subject unto Christ, so let the wives be to their own husbands in every thing. (25) Husbands, love your wives, even as Christ also loved the church, and gave himself for it; (26) That he might sanctify and cleanse it with the washing of water by the word, (27) That he might present it to himself a glorious church, not having spot, or wrinkle, or any such thing; but that it should be holy and without blemish. (28) So ought men to love their wives as their own bodies. He that loveth his wife loveth himself. (29) For no man ever yet hated his own flesh; but nourisheth and cherisheth it, even as the Lord the church: (30) For we are members of his body, of his flesh, and of his bones. (31) For this cause shall a man leave his father and mother, and shall be joined unto his wife, and they two shall be one flesh. (32) This is a great mystery: but I speak concerning Christ and the church. (33) Nevertheless let every one of you in particular so love his wife even as himself; and the wife see that she reverence her husband."*

The Nature of this Subordination

This subordination does not involve personal character. Nowhere in scripture is there a slightest hint that the ladies are inferior to the men concerning personal character. It is admitted that many of the men within and without the church have abused their wives in this area, and I appreciate the opportunity to set things right. Our ladies of the church are to be applauded and upheld as their honesty, integrity, and patience are demonstrated to be superior to that of most men; as well as, in many other areas such as endurance, gentleness, unselfishness, ministering to the suffering, etc. Women excel over the men, and we men could learn from them. Many women have qualities few men can attain to.

I have a tremendous dependency upon my wife. So much so that I feel that I could not continue without her. This dependency exists because of the qualities God has put in her. This dependency also helps bond our home together.

This subordination touches not the question of salvation. *"There is neither Jew nor Greek, there is neither bond nor free, there is neither male nor female: for ye are all one in Christ Jesus."* Galatians 3:28. This verse has so frequently been misused and misapplied to teach equality in all matters. This verse then has been taken out of its natural context. We are taught that there is no nationality, or sect of people, or sex of humanity, that is outside of the love of Christ.

Nor is this a question of ability. Many are very good at things they ought not to do. Ability or success is not a criteria for what is right. While Moses was successful in obtaining water by striking the rock the second time, yet he kindled the anger of God and sealed his death before entering the Promised Land. Numbers 20:11-12. The anti-Christ is going to be successful in leading the ungodly into apostasy and idolatry. II Thessalonians 2:1-11 and Revelations 13:3-8.

This then is not a lower position than that of the men but rather a matter of rank. The President of our great country is not greater in character, intelligence, or ability then many Americans, yet he out ranks them. We aren't inferior to him in any way except in authority, and I don't feel threatened, abused, or put down in any way. The ladies are to submit to their husband's authority the same way the men submit to Christ, and Christ to the Father. I Corinthians 11:3.

Today the world is crying for rights as it never has before and as time goes on this cry will only increase. Yet we seem to be losing more rights with each passing day. We miss the mark when we seek equal rights. The real question isn't equal rights, but rather equal duties. We have only two rights given to us by our Heavenly Father. They being the right to worship and obey Him. For these are rights we will soon put our lives on the line to defend. All other rights (as good as they are) were given to us by man, and by man they shall be taken away.

This is humbling both to the men and the women. To the woman because she must submit to her husband and to the men because of the tremendous responsibility placed in his hands.

How does this subordination reflect on the women of the church? Paul refers to this subject and says:

> I Timothy 2:11-12 *"Let the woman learn in silence with all subjection. (12) But I suffer not a woman to teach, nor to usurp authority over the man, but to be in silence."* I Corinthians 14:34-35 *"Let your women keep silence in the churches: for it is not permitted unto them to speak; but they are commanded to be under obedience, as also saith the law. (35) And if they will learn anything, let them ask their husbands at home: for it is a shame for women to speak in the church."*

It is my personal opinion that this "SPEAKING" is having reference to publicly addressing the church body—such as giving devotions, preaching, teaching, testimonies, and song leading of a mixed congregation of both men and women. That would be exercising authority over the man, and is strictly forbidden by scripture. Paul instructs the ladies of the church that they speak not a word even to the point that any inquiry or the giving of information must be done through their husband, or at least a man of the church. This is true even in public prayer. I Timothy 2:8a. *"I will therefore that MEN pray every where . . ."* Luke 18:1b *". . . that men ought always to pray, and not to faint;"* (Emphasis mine LD)

The obligation, duty and privilege of leading a church body in prayer rest upon the men of the church. This in no way implies that the women are not to pray, but that they pray privately and not to lead the church in public prayer. Read also I Corinthians 11:13.

The question of the women preaching is also not forgotten in scripture; first noticing the requirements of an elder. *"If a MAN desires the office of a bishop, HE desireth a good work. A bishop then must be blameless, the HUSBAND of one wife."* I Timothy 3:1-2 (Emphasis mine L.D.) Couple this together with the instructions of the women being silent and not teaching, makes filling the pulpit an impossible idea.

The last question posed is that of the deacon. Again, noticing the requirements of a deacon given in I Timothy 3:8-13 *the HUSBAND of one wife.* Also, in Acts 6:3 this position was given to MEN full of the Holy Spirit. Acts 6:3 *"Wherefore, brethren, look ye out among you seven MEN of honest report, full of the Holy Ghost and wisdom, whom we many appoint over this business."* (Emphasis mine L.D.)

Ladies, I've addressed six things you cannot scripturally do in a mixed assembly of the church. You can't speak, teach, preach, pray publicly, lead a congregation, or hold the office of a deacon. However, what you can do is by far too numerous to mention. The condition of the church is in the hands of the men, but the condition of the men is in hands of their wives. Time simply will not permit me to elaborate further on the privileges, responsibilities, and obligations that are ours. I hope you will now look beyond your pride, and go on seeking to glorify God by submitting yourself to your husband, encouraging your husband to submit to Christ, and thereby obeying Holy writ.

How does this subordination reflect on the women in the home? Equal authority in the home as well as in the church is an enticing scheme of the evil one. Equal authority in the home means difficult problems that cannot be resolved. Equal authority produces disagreements, bitterness, hatred, envy, strife and finally a broken home. In order for a home to remain sound there must be a head of the house, and scripture places that squarely on the man of the house.

> I Corinthians 11:3 *"But I would have you know, that the head of every man is Christ; and the head of the woman is the man; and Head of Christ is God."* I Peter 3:1 *"Likewise, ye wives, be in subjection to your own husbands; that, if any obey not the word, they also may with out the word be won by conversion of the wives:"* I Peter 3:8 *"Finally, be ye all of one mind, having compassion one of another, love as brethren, be pitiful, be courteous:"*

One mind also has reference to one head; imagine if you will two heads of the home with equal authority, but separate minds. From where would come a solution to a disagreement? Perhaps after a physical confrontation, to the victor goes the spoils, or to the one who has the fastest draw, or the biggest gun. God forbid. There must be a head of the house to finalize a discussion, and to end a conflict.

The Reason for this Subordination

This subordination had its origin in the creation. I Corinthians 11:8-9 *"For the man is not of the woman; but woman of the man. (9) Neither was the man created for the woman; but the woman for the man."* This subordination is a design of God the Father, the creator of all creation. It had its beginning in the Garden. Genesis 2:18 *"And the Lord God said it is not good that the man should be alone; I will make him an help meet for him."*

Reading again in I Corinthians 11:8-9. *"For the man is not of the woman; but the woman of the man. (9) Neither was the man created for the woman; but the woman for the man."* I Timothy 2:13-14 *"For Adam was first formed, then Eve."* (14) *"And Adam was not deceived, but the woman being deceived was in the transgression."* Genesis 3:16 *"Unto the woman he said, I will greatly multiply thy sorrow and thy conception; in sorrow thou shalt bring forth children; and thy desire shall be to thy husband, and he shall rule over thee."* I Peter 3:7 *"Likewise, ye husbands, dwell with them according to knowledge, giving honour unto the wife, as unto the weaker vessel, and as being heirs together of the grace of life; that your prayers be not hindered."*

God created the human race according to his own sovereign will, and according to His own purpose within himself. However, let us men remember that women being a weaker vessel in no way strips the ladies of their due honor.

This teaching isn't a popular one, but the truth of God never has been popular in the world system. God never has been swayed by popular opinion, nor governed by public demand.

The Symbol of their Subordination

The fact of the subordination of the woman to man is divinely appointed, and this truth is symbolized in two ways, by the women keeping their hair long, and by wearing a veil covering when praying or during the preaching of the word.

I Corinthians 11:5-6 *"But every woman that prayeth or prophesieth with her head uncovered dishonoureth her head; for that is even all one as if she were shaven. (6) For if the woman be not covered, let her also be shorn; but if it be a shame for a woman to be shorn or shaven, let her be covered."*

First: considering the hair. I Corinthians 11:15 *"But if a woman have long hair, it is glory to her: for her hair is given her for a covering."*

This long hair is a glory to her while in the preceding verse the men are admonished to keep their hair short. Certainly the question must have occurred to the reader, what is considered to be long hair and what is considered as short hair? One thing is safe to assume. The women's hair must be longer than the men's, and the men's hair must be shorter than the women's. In today's society the reverse is common place. It's especially sad in our churches. We then wonder why our churches lack the power that they once enjoyed. Have we gotten so lax that obedience to scripture is no-longer the rule? Disobedience robs God of His glory, and the church of their power. For the sake of numbers have we begun tickling the ears of those who were once taught sound doctrine?

Then the veil covering comes into question. It is a truth that one cannot dogmatically teach a cardinal doctrine on one passage of scripture. Therefore, we can't go off the deep end into fanaticism. However, it is also a truth that we cannot avoid this teaching as many seem to do. Paul plainly teaches that the head covering for the women or the lack of a covering is directly related to their submitting to their head. (Husband)

Let's make some observations as we closely examine scripture. I Corinthians 11:4-5a *"Every man praying or prophesying, having his head covered, dishonoureth his head (Christ). (5a) But every woman that prayeth or prophesieth with her head uncovered dishonoureth her head (husband):"*

Therefore the man's head is to remain uncovered, and the ladies head is to be covered. Dually noted is verse 15 *"... for her hair is given her for a covering."* But is this hair the same covering that is spoken of in verses 4 and 5? If so, then the men must have shaven heads (no hair). Also verse 5 would not be understandable or teachable. For the sake of argument let's consider this verse with the covering being the hair, and then let's paraphrase it into every day English. (If the women have no hair, let her also have short hair: but if it is a shame for a woman to have short hair or no hair, let her have hair.) Is it possible for her to have short hair and no hair at the same time? This verse is then not understandable, and not teachable. Now let's paraphrase this same verse with the covering being a veil. (If the women be not veiled, let her also have short hair: but it is a shame for a woman to have short hair, or no hair, let her put on a veil.) This verse now is understandable and teachable. It makes sense and is a complete thought. Therefore, the covering in verses 4 and 5 must not be the hair, and must be some other type of covering. A veil then is a symbol of the woman's subjection to her husband provided of course she truly is in subjection. To not be in subjection and to wear a veil is to deceive the church.

I believe it to be wrong for a church to <u>dogmatically</u> teach this, or to <u>require</u> the women of the church to wear a covering during any service of the church as we have no other New Testament teaching on this subject. Therefore it should be encouraged by the church, but left to the individual members to work this out among themselves.

It is my earnest and prayerful desire that you will weigh out what I've said against scripture, and allow scripture to be your only rule of faith, order, and practice.

CHAPTER 14

Difficulties of Pentecostalism

My heart is saddened and greatly troubled for many that have fallen headlong into the snare of the devil. The Pentecostal persuasion has overtaken them and their charisma has enslaved them. They are also referred to as the charismatic movement. Once snared into this stronghold of Satan it is very difficult to set them free. It is for this reason that I will attempt to set in order the teachings of God's word concerning this subject.

First, allow me to clarify a proper view of God's word. The bible is the final authority in all matters of faith, order, and practice. Do you believe that? If you faultier on that point, you need not read any further. You've made up your mind and scriptural truth means little or nothing to you. However, if you will set aside your own personal prejudices, and center on God's word you can learn what the mind of Christ is concerning this important subject. Remember always that the flesh and the spirit are opposed to each other.

Galatians 5:17 *"For the flesh lusteth against the Spirit, and the Spirit against the flesh: and these are contrary the one to the other: so that ye cannot do the things that ye would."*

To find the mind of Christ in this matter we must set aside all prejudice views and enticements of the flesh.

If I am successful in showing you in God's word that this Pentecostal movement of speaking in an unknown tongue is not of God, or the Holy Spirit, but of another spirit entirely. Will you than abandon it and search out Christ's true churches? That is the question, and that is your choice. We've heard it said the proof is in the pudding. Well, the pudding here is God's word.

I John 4:1 *"Beloved, believe not every spirit, but try the spirits whether they are of God: because many false prophets are gone out into the world."*

It is so easy to follow the flesh, and be enticed and overcome by it. Therefore I have listed some scriptures which deal with this subversion of the flesh.

- Matthew 26:41 *"The spirit indeed is willing, but the flesh is weak."*
- John 6:63 *"The flesh profiteth nothing"*
- Romans 7:18 *"For I know that in me, (that is, in my flesh) dwelleth no good thing."*
- Romans 8:1 *". . . who walk not after the flesh, but after the Spirit."*
- Romans 8:8 *"So then they that are in the flesh cannot please God."*
- Romans 8:13 *"For if ye live after the flesh, ye shall die: but if ye through the Spirit do mortify the deeds of the body, ye shall live."*
- Romans 13:14 *". . . make no provision for the flesh, to fulfill the lusts thereof."*
- I Cor. 1:29 *"That no flesh should glory in his presence."*
- Gal. 2:16 *". . . by the works of the law shall no flesh be justified."*
- Philippians 3:3 *". . . have no confidence in the flesh."*

Many more scriptures could be cited, but these should be sufficient to show us our need of mortifying the deeds of the flesh rather than following them. I've had many good intentioned people say "you don't know how I felt", or "oh how good it feels". First let me say, I do know how they feel, I felt it as well. In my earlier days as a Christian, I experienced these same feelings of the flesh and was nearly enticed by them. Secondly and more importantly, it doesn't matter how we feel. How good it feels is not the acid test of its truthfulness. We are admonished to try the spirits to see if they are truly of God. It's how they line up with God's word that matters. I agree that these people are being led by a spirit, just not God's spirit. I'm not saying this to be disrespectful to anyone. Outside of comparing this with God's word it would be impossible to tell what spirit it is. Thus comparing it to scripture is vital in determining its truthfulness.

Again I ask you, do you really want to know the truth or would you rather just not know and keep on trucking as you have been?

The gifts of the early churches are recorded in Mark 16:17-18 and 1Corithians 12-14. Read these verses over many times and become very familiar with them. Remember what Paul said to Timothy concerning God's word.

II Timothy 3:16-17 *"All scripture is given by inspiration of God, and is profitable for doctrine, for reproof, for correction, for instruction in righteousness: (17) That the man of God may be perfect (matured), throughly furnished unto all good works."* (Emphasis mine L.D.)

We don't add, or subtract from God's word. We don't skip over or neglect what we don't like or doesn't fit our fancy, nor do we clasp onto what we like at the expense of the contexts.

It was around the turn of the century in or about 1900 or 1901 that the Pentecostal charismatic movement had its beginning. Its growth was very rapid mainly because their charismatic movement was so likable to the flesh. Whenever you give to others what they like, they will keep coming, and bring others with them.

Their faith is a faith based on the feelings of the flesh. Physical feelings are encouraged over scripture. They use a certain portion of scripture, and base the foundation of their church on it at the expense of the true context, rather than the whole of God's word.

Acts 20:27 Paul said, *"For I have not shunned to declare unto you ALL the counsel of God,"* (Emphasis mine L.D.)

The leaders of this church and churches have taken the day of Pentecost in Acts 2, and Mark's instruction in Mark 16:17-18, and Apostle Paul's instructions of I Corinthians 12-14 and based their churches around them forgetting and ignoring the rest of Holy writ. Even in these scriptures they have taken out of context supposing these gifts are to be for today.

The gifts and miracles, and wonders were given to the church as signs during the infancy of the church, and until the rest of the cannon of scripture was completed.

> I Corinthians 14:22 *"Wherefore tongues ARE FOR A SIGN, not to them that believe, but to them that believe not: but prophesying (preaching) serveth not for them that believe not, but for them which believe."* (Emphasis mine L.D.)

These gifts were meant for a sign to the early church in our history. The early church needed these special gifts to accredit and authenticate both the Apostles and the church as being from God. These newly converted saints needed confirmation that the apostles and the church were what the apostles said they were.

Also, the cannon of scripture had not yet been completed so they needed extra and special guidance from the apostles. These new converts needed extra confirmation that the messages they were hearing were actually from God. Paul was defending his apostleship against both non-believers and believers who were questioning his authority.

Not many of us will disagree with the notion that the apostleship is no longer with us. That office is done away with. Why should we then hesitate to believe that the special gifts also should be done away with? When the bible was completed, the apostleship ceased, and the church is more matured. There remains no need for the apostles, special gifts or special miracles

> Hebrews 2:3-4 *"How shall we escape, if we neglect so great salvation; which at the first began to be spoken by the Lord, and was confirmed unto us by them that heard him; (4) God also bearing them witness, both with signs and wonders, and with divers miracles, and gifts of the Holy Ghost, according to his own will?"*

Romans 10:2 *"For I bear record that they have a zeal of God, BUT NOT ACCORDING TO KNOWLEDGE."* (Emphasis mine L.D.)

Everyone desires peace, even if it's a worldly peace. But worldly peace isn't the peace given by Christ.

John 14:27 *"Peace I leave with you, my peace I give unto you: not as the world giveth, give I unto you. Let not your heart be troubled, neither let it be afraid."*

Philippians 4:7 *"And the peace of God, which passeth all understanding, shall keep your hearts and minds through Christ Jesus."*

The peace given by Christ is not a worldly peace that will pass away from one day to the next. It's an abiding peace that endures through time. It's a "peace" that is according to knowledge of God's word that stands ready at all times. This peace that cannot be explained or described is a peace that can only be experienced within the inner man. Not an outer experience but an inner experience. The Pentecostal experience is solely an outer man's experience. This inner peace of God doesn't need an outward exhibition of a worldly outburst of physical exhaustion. Neither is it an outward show to others of your spirituality. This peace of God always comes with knowledge of God, and not merely the fleshly feelings of the outer man through the indwelling of the Holy Spirit.

When the apostles had left the scene and the bible canon was complete, the special gifts, and miracles of Mark 16:17-18 had ceased. They no longer were needed.

I Corinthians 13:10-11 *"But when that which is perfect (complete) is come, then that which is in part shall be done away. (11) When I was a child, I spake as a child, I understood as a child, I thought as a child: but when I became a man, I put away childish things."* (Emphasis mine L.D.)

Pentecostalism has made several errors that make them less than scriptural.

1. Their ancestry dates their beginning around 1900 which is nineteen hundred years after Christ instituted his church.

   Matthew 16:18 Jesus said, *"I will build my church."*

   Jesus built his church during his earthly ministry on earth, and that wasn't in the year of 1900 A.D. This alone disqualifies them from ever claiming to be Christ's church.

2. Pentecostals place an over emphasis on human experiences even to the point where it's above God's word. Appealing to the flesh is not a criterion of God's truth. In fact, the opposite is usually the case. The flesh loves to be glorified rather than to glorify God. They are more willing to trust their feelings rather than God's word. They let their heart decide truth. Consider what Jeremiah says about that.

   Jeremiah 17:9 *"The heart is deceitful above all things, and desperately wicked: who can know it?"*

3. Pentecostalism places a greater emphasis of worship on the Holy Spirit rather than on our Lord and Saviour Jesus Christ. Much is said about the baptism of the Holy Spirit, and the gifts of the spirit. Even to the point of worshipping the Holy Spirit.

   The third person of the God-head (Holy Spirit) never seeks his own worship, but seeks rather to worship and glorify Jesus Christ.

   John 16:13-14 Jesus speaking, *"Howbeit when he, the spirit of truth, is come, he will guide you unto all truth:* FOR HE SHALL NOT SPEAK OF HIMSELF; BUT WHATSOEVER HE SHALL HEAR, THAT SHALL HE SPEAK: *and he will show you things to come.* (14) HE SHALL GLORIFY ME (CHRIST): *for he shall receive of mine, and shall show it unto you."* (Emphasis mine LD)

This is much like a good, faithful and obedient wife continually encouraging and building her husband and never herself. A good wife is likened unto the Holy Spirit of the home. The main function of the Holy Spirit is to glorify Christ, and never himself. He draws attention to Christ and for Christ that in all things Christ may have the preeminence.

Colossians 1:18 *"And he is the head of the body, the church: who is the beginning, the firstborn from the dead; that in* ALL THINGS HE MIGHT HAVE THE PRE-EMINENCE." (Emphasis mine LD)

We are to be filled with the Holy Spirit, be led, taught and obey the leadership of the Holy Spirit, but worship and glorify Christ.

The baptism of the Holy Spirit was a onetime event. The church was empowered by the Holy Spirit and baptized in the Holy Spirit. This never was repeated nor ever will be repeated. Just as a new child of God needs one time to be baptized by immersion in water, so the church only needed to be baptized in the Holy Spirit once and for all time.

Ephesians 4:5 *"One Lord, one faith, one baptism . . ."*

It is when we are spirit filled that we are also Christ centered.

What is it that causes supposed Christians to seek to edify and glorify the flesh? The answer is the flesh itself. Men seek self-glorification, and the attention of others.

Another concern concerning the worshipping desires of the flesh. The flesh loves physical worship supposing this is true worship. However, God will not accept physical worship or rituals coming from the flesh.

John 4:23-24 *"But the hour cometh and now is, when true worshippers shall worship the Father in spirit and in truth: For the Father seeketh such to worship him. (24) God is a spirit; and they that worship him must worship him in spirit and in truth."*

Even during the early times of the church. Paul set restrictions concerning these gifts and the exercising of them.

1. Paul said he would rather speak five understandable words rather than ten thousand words in an unknown tongue.

    I Corinthians 14:19 *"Yet in the church I had rather speak five words with my understanding, that by my voice I might teach others also, than ten thousand words in an unknown tongue."*

2. Speaking in an unknown tongue never could edify the church. Only the one doing the speaking would be edified.

    I Corinthians 14:4 *"He that speaketh in an unknown tongue edifieth himself; but he that prophesieth edifieth the church."*

3. No one could speak in an unknown tongue unless an interpreter was present. I Corinthians 14:28 *"But if there be no interpreter, let him keep silence in the church; and let him speak to himself, and to God."*

4. Never more than two or three during an entire service. I Corinthians 14:27 *"If any man speak in an unknown tongue, let it be by two, or at the most by three, and that by course; and let one interpret."*

5. Never by a woman because women are to remain silent during service. I Corinthians 14:34-35 *"Let your women keep silence in the churches: for it is not permitted unto them to speak; but they are commanded to be under obedience, as also saith the law. (35) And if they will learn anything let them ask their husbands at home: for it is a shame for women to speak in the church."* also in I Timothy 2:11-12 *"Let the woman learn in silence with all subjection. But I suffer not a woman to teach, nor to usurp authority over the man, but to be in silence."*

Most of us have witnessed these services where most or all of these have been violated. They then claim "what a spirit filled service". This may be a spirit but not God's spirit. God will never lead or do anything contrary to his word. "*. . . believe not every spirit, but try the spirits, whether they are of God:*" I John 4:1

CHAPTER 15

Traditions, Lies, and Hypocrisies

It is with great sadness of heart that I feel that I must try to make corrections amongst many of my brethren in Christ. I say this as politely as I possibly can. I must however realize that to many of which I am now addressing will be offended, and still others are not my brethren in Christ at all. This is disturbing to me. Many wolves in sheep's clothing have entered into the churches not sparing the flock, and have and are perverting the Gospel of Christ.

As a result many false doctrines are being taught, and many of God's children are being persuaded to believe doctrines that are completely foreign to scripture. Easy believism, the free agency of man and the universal, invisible church comes to mind. Also false traditions that have been passed down through the ages are treated as doctrine. All are tactics of Satan to hinder God's truth and Christ's church.

Pastors, preachers, and lay-men that have never tasted that the Lord is gracious are leading astray the saints of God by the droves. Newborn babes in Christ are gullible to their persuasion.

These are false teachers, and will one day be dealt with by a just and wrathful God. Until then they need to be exposed by those of us who truly do love the Lord and the truth of his word. Standing for truth at times requires falsehoods to be exposed.

Ephesians 6:11-13, *"Put on the whole armour of God, that ye may be able to stand against the wiles of the devil. (12) For we wrestle not against flesh and blood, but against principalities, against powers, against the rulers of the darkness of this world, against spiritual wickedness in high places. (13) Wherefore take unto you the whole armour of God, that ye may be able to withstand in the evil day, and having done all, to stand."*

Verse 13 *"Having done all"* includes exposing untruths. Then stand and stand boldly.

In this writing I will seek to expose evil traditions, and hypocrisies of men both unintentional and intentional.

Traditions

The flesh loves traditions, mainly because these traditions had their start with the joys of the flesh. Most of what transpires within the worship service of the church service today has had its roots in tradition. It's been done this way for centuries, and who are we to change it now. My parents, grandparents and great grand parents have done it this way, and it seemed good for them. The idea is if it was good for them it must be good for us.

Traditions aren't necessarily bad. It depends on the tradition and where it comes from, and where it leads to. There are certain traditions that spring from scripture. These are good and should be kept and continued. These have God as their author, and are found in the golden pages of scripture. Still others come from the vanity of men who are controlled by the flesh. It is to these traditions that I write. These have no Biblical warrant, and look to the flesh for their origin.

I think it would be good for a short study of what the scripture says about the flesh.

Matthew 26:41, *"The spirit indeed is willing but the flesh is weak."*

John 6:63, *"The flesh profiteth nothing."*

Romans 7:18, *"In me; that is, in my flesh, dwelleth no good thing."*

Romans 8:8, *"So then they that are in the flesh cannot please God."*

Many more scriptures could be produced on this subject however this should suffice. It's a plain and simple truth that the flesh cannot determine scriptural truth. Consider also what Jeremiah has to say of the heart.

Jeremiah17:9, *"The heart is deceitful above all things, and desperately wicked: who can know it?"*

I have a real hard time with people who (even though they won't say it) believe God is not serious about what He says. I've heard them say, God is just exaggerating the point. That's to say God is not truthful. People just can't put the flesh aside and believe God's word, Christians and non-Christians alike. Sad isn't it? I think the very first thing one will learn after departing from this world will be **God meant exactly what He said.** The heart is the last thing we should be following in our worldly adventures. It's easy to believe what the flesh likes and hard to believe what the flesh doesn't like. Man's basis of determining right from wrong is the feelings of the heart. Strange isn't it. Man goes to the most unaccredited and deceitful source of our being, to determine what is and what isn't truth. It's the flesh that will usually determine the traditions we either keep or leave behind.

Matthew 15:2-3 *"Why do thy disciples transgress the tradition of the elders? for they wash not their hands when they eat bread. (3) But He answered and said unto them, Why do ye also transgress the commandment of God by your tradition?"*

Matthew 15:6, *"Thus have ye made the commandment of God of none effect by your tradition."*

Mark7:7-9, *"Howbeit in vain do they worship me, teaching for doctrines the commandments of men. (8) For laying aside the commandment of God, ye hold the tradition of men, as the washing of pots and cups: and many other such like things ye do. (9) And he said unto them, Full well ye reject the commandment of God, that ye may keep your own tradition."*

Mark 7:13, *"Making the word of God of none effect through your tradition,"*

Colossians 2:8 *"Beware lest any man spoil you through philosophy and vain deceit, after the tradition of men, after the rudiments of the world, and not after Christ."*

I Peter 1:18, *"Forasmuch as ye know that ye were not redeemed with corruptible things, as silver and gold, from your vain conversation received by tradition from your fathers;"*

Man has so perverted God's plan of salvation and God's perfect will for man in his service to God that men are completely left in the dark, and have no understanding as to seeking or pleasing God. Man within himself has no knowledge of God, or no desire to come to know Him. They are misled by traditions into believing they are doing God a service.

That's not to say all traditions are bad. Traditions taught in scripture and practiced by the disciples have scriptural warrant and need to be practiced.

II Thessalonians 3:6, *"Now we command you, brethren, in the name of our Lord Jesus Christ, that ye withdraw yourselves from every brother that walketh disorderly, and not after the tradition which he received of us."*

I will and do follow the traditions that have scriptural warrant, and leave behind all traditions that do not.

Now, this should open up a whole new can of worms to which I shall be scorned at for many a day. First allow me to make one clarification. However, what I'm about to address is my very strongly held opinion. I don't look down or badly at anyone who doesn't agree with me on these points.

These traditions consist of Christmas, Easter, Halloween, and Valentine's Day. The world claims these to be religious celebrations, but history and scripture don't agree. These are celebrations held over, and rescued from Babylon, the not-so great. The same that God called mystery Babylon, the mother of harlots, and abominations of the earth. Revelation 17:5. Known first as the tower of Babel in Genesis 11, Babylon was founded by Nimrod. Babylon had many celebrations that worshipped false gods and angered God to the point that He confounded their language and dispersed them around the world.

They had an early spring, early summer, fall, and winter celebrations. The first celebration worshipped a false god called cupid. [A love god] Then they had a fertility god which they celebrated with eggs. An egg was supposed to come down from heaven and land in the Euphrates River where the fish rolled it to the shore and then the birds of the air came to hatch the egg. When the egg hatched the queen of heaven [Ishtar] was hatched. She was the wife of Nimrod. The winter celebration was the birth of their son, Tammuz. He was born on our December 25th. He was celebrated as a god and his birthday celebration began on the eve of his birthday and lasted for twelve days. This celebration consisted of a merry man dressed in a red suit and giving gifts to children of good behavior. A tree was chopped down and decorated with silver and gold. (Jeremiah 10:1-5.) They had their mistletoes and wreaths. They sang songs and made merry, yes, they celebrated the birth of a boy child, but it wasn't Jesus, and wasn't in Bethlehem. They also had a fall celebration in which they practiced witchcraft.

Now, we know that Jesus wasn't born in December as this was too cold for Joseph and Mary to make the trip to Bethlehem to be taxed. This was done in the fall of the year after the harvest. Also the shepherds were not in the fields after the last of October. Why then do you suppose December was selected for this celebration???

It's completely natural to believe that when God dispersed them around the world they took with them their traditions and customs just as we would today. This was ingrained into them just as Christmas is to most people today.

Then along came Constantine, a man that tried to rule the world. But could he get the Christians to follow him? He knew he had to make believe it was a Christian thing to do. So, He changed the names to protect the guilty. He added Christ's name to all the heathen practices from Babylon to make it appear Christian. He was either Christianizing paganism, or paganizing Christendom. I'm not sure which, but both are wrong.

Ezekiel 20:39 *"Pollute ye my holy name no more with your gifts, and with your idols."*

Immature Christians can be very gullible and easily lead astray. The traditions of men can be deceptive to deceitful hearts, and lead people by the millions or even billions right to the gates of hell. All the while thinking they are doing God a service.

Lies and Hypocracies

I've learned a very hard lesson, one that I didn't like to learn. Students of the Bible will never agree completely on theology, but certain truths will and should become evident over the years. This should be enough to convince them of certain truths that should change their teachings on certain doctrines, such as God's plan of salvation. Are we saved by works, or by grace through faith? Scripture is too plan about this, and the matter is too important to be wrong. For example, those who say they believe in salvation by grace through faith and then add baptism, morality, church membership, or any other such thing are themselves deceiving others knowingly and intentionally.

Paul said it this way.

Romans 11:6, *"And if by grace, then is it no more of works: otherwise grace is no more grace. But if it be of works, then is it no more grace: otherwise work is no more work."*

Ephesians 2:8-9 *"For by grace are ye saved through faith; and that not of yourselves: it is the Gift of God: (9) Not of works, lest any man should boast."*

I was raised in a protestant church for the first twenty five years of my life, and believed all was well. It wasn't until I was introduced to some truths I had never heard before. I heard the truth of salvation, the truth of being born again. Such things I'd never heard before. Why is it I never heard these before? How important are these truths? How thankful am I that some Christians came into my life that cared enough about me to go out of their way to tell me what I needed to know, such as the truth of God's plan of salvation. It was Jesus that said *"Except a man be born again he cannot see the kingdom of God."* This truth was being withheld from me for twenty five years. I was to them a number on a membership roll. At first I thought they were only mistaken, but after many years I came to realize their lack of concern. My ears were being tickled just to keep me coming back.

The Apostle Paul, warned us of this time we are now living in.

II Timothy 3:1-7 & 13 *"This know also, that in the last days perilous times shall come. (2) For men shall be lovers of their own selves, covetous, boasters, proud, blasphemers, disobedient to parents, unthankful, unholy, (3) Without natural affection, trucebreakers, false accusers, incontinent, fierce, despisers of those that are good. (4) Traitors, heady highminded, lovers of pleasures more than lovers of God; (5) Having a form of godliness, but denying the power thereof: from such turn away."* (13) *But evil men and seducers shall wax worse and worse, deceiving, and being deceived."*

II Timothy 4:3-5, *"For the time will come when they will not endure sound doctrine; but after their own lusts shall they heap to themselves teachers, having itching ears; (4) And they shall turn away their ears from the truth, and shall be turned unto fables. (5) But watch thou in all things, endure afflictions, do the work of an evangelist, make full proof of thy ministry."*

Certainly, we are living in the last days where pastors and preachers within churches are seeking to please the populous for the sake of numbers. They think the larger the churches the more successful their ministry. These are soothsayers who would tickle the ears of their hearers. All are at the expense of the truth and the souls of their parishioners.

It was after the realization of this fact that I appreciated and loved the truth of God's word. I despise, and detest those lies and the hypocrites that told them. Those preachers teach doctrines right out of hell. Doctrines like, smile God loves you. These lies will destroy and rob from you the fear of God.

The idea is, God loves everybody, and Jesus died for everybody, therefore every ones sins are paid and everyone will go to heaven. That's a lie right from Satan's mouth. The facts are, God doesn't love everybody and Jesus didn't die for everybody.

John 5:21b, "*. . . even so the Son quickeneth whom he will.*"

John 6:37-39, "*All that the Father giveth me shall come to me; and him that cometh to me I will in no wise cast out. (38) For I came down from heaven, not to do mine own will, but the will of him that sent me. (39) And this is the Father's will which hath sent me, that of all which he hath given me I should lose nothing, but should raise it up again at the last day.*"

John 6:65, "*And he said, Therefore said I unto you, that no man can come unto me, except it were given unto him of my Father.*"

John 10:11, "*I am the good shepherd: the good shepherd giveth his life for the sheep.*" (Sheep only, emphasis mine L.D.)

John 10:14-16, *"I am the good shepherd, and know my sheep, and am known of mine. (15) As the Father knoweth me, even so know I the Father: and I lay down my life for the sheep. (16) And other sheep I have, which are not of this fold: them also I must bring, and they shall hear my voice; and there shall be one fold, and one shepherd."*

John 10:26-29 *"But ye believe not, because ye are not of my sheep, as I said unto you. (27) My sheep hear my voice, and I know them, and they follow me: (28) And I give unto them eternal life; and they shall never perish, neither shall any man pluck them out of my hand. (29) My Father, which gave them me, is greater then all; and no man is able to pluck them out of my Fathers hand."*

John 13:1c *". . . having loved his own which were in the world, he loved them unto the end."*

John 15:16, *"Ye have not chosen me, but I have chosen you, and ordained you, that ye should go and bring forth fruit, and that your fruit should remain: and that whatsoever ye shall ask of the Father in my name, he may give it you."*

John 17:2, 6-7, 9, 11 and 20, *"As thou hast given him power over all flesh, that he should give eternal life to as many as thou hast given him. (6) I have manifested thy name unto the men which thou gavest me out of the world: thine they were, and thou gavest them me; and they have kept thy word. (7) Now they have known that all things whatsoever thou hast given me are of thee. (9) I pray for them: I pray not for the world, but for them which thou hast given me; for they are thine. (11) And now I am no more in the world, but these are in the world, and I come to thee, Holy Father, keep through thine own name those whom thou hast given me, that they may be one, as we are. (20) Neither pray I for these alone, but for them also which shall believe on me through their word."*

Revelation 3:19 says, God rebukes or chastens all that He loves *"As many as I love, I rebuke and chasten:"*

Hebrews 12:6-8, reveals that God doesn't rebuke everyone. Therefore, so He must not love everyone.

This false doctrine that teaches that God loves everyone removes the fear of God from people's lives, and gives them a false sense of security.

John 3:16, is perhaps the most quoted of all scripture and also the most misunderstood scripture in the entire Bible. Jesus is speaking to Nicodemus, a ruler of the Jews. The Jews were of the opinion that salvation was only of the Jews, and for good reason. In the Old Testament salvation was of the Jews. Jesus is now telling Nicodemus that God's love is now worldwide in scope. God's love does no longer stop at the boarders of Israel. God's love now encompasses every nation, every kindred, and every tongue. Ask yourself how many Gentiles were saved in the Old Testament? His love is now international in scope, but not necessarily every person.

John 4:22, *"Ye worship ye know not what: we know what we worship: for salvation is of the Jews."* (Jesus was speaking of Old Testament times)

Romans 3:29, *"Is he the God of the Jews only? is he not also of the Gentiles? Yes, of the Gentiles also:"*

Romans 9:13, *"As it is written, Jacob have I loved, but Esau have I hated."*

Malachi 1:2-3, *"I have loved you, saith the LORD. Yet ye say, Wherein hast thou loved us? Was not Esau Jacob's brother? saith the LORD: yet I loved Jacob. (3) And I hated Esau, and laid his mountains, and his heritage waste for the dragons of the wilderness."*

Israel was, and is God's chosen nation. Although God has temporarily withdrawn from Israel, He has chosen a certain number of Gentiles. It's interesting to note that many don't object to God choosing a nation, but do object to God choosing certain individuals. Yet nations are made up of individuals. During the Old Testament God chose a certain number of the Jews, and in the New Testament God chose a certain number of the Gentiles. Today the Gentiles that are chosen of God are being graphed into the olive tree, and are children of Abraham by faith, and are counted as the seed of Abraham.

> Galatians 3:7-9, 14, and 29, "*Know ye therefore that they which are of faith, the same are the children of Abraham. (8) And the scripture, foreseeing that God would justify the heathen through faith, preached before the gospel unto Abraham, saying, In thee shall all nations be blessed. (9) So then they which be of faith are blessed with faithful Abraham.*" (14) *That the blessing of Abraham might come on the Gentiles through Jesus Christ; that we might receive the promise of the Spirit through faith. (29) And if ye be Christ's, then are ye Abraham's seed, and heirs according to the promise.*"

We who are living by faith are all the children of Abraham, and heirs according to the promise of Abraham. That makes all true believers in Christ, spiritual Jews.

We are then to conclude that God, before the creation of this world, set his love on a certain and a chosen number of both Jews and Gentiles, and in the course of time will bring them to a place of salvation through Jesus Christ our Lord and Saviour.

> Ephesians 1:4-5, "*According as he hath chosen us in him before the foundation of the world, that we should be holy and without blame before him in love: (5) Having predestinated us unto the adoption of children by Jesus Christ to himself, according to the good pleasure of his will.*"

Romans 9:15-23, *"For he saith to Moses, I will have mercy on whom I will have mercy, and I will have compassion on whom I will have compassion. (16) So then it is, not of him that willeth, nor him that runneth, but of God that sheweth mercy. (17) For the scripture saith unto Pharaoh, Even for this same purpose have I raised thee up, that I might shew my power in thee, and that my name might be declared throughout all the earth. (18) Therefore hath he mercy on whom he will have mercy, and whom he will he hardeneth. (19) Thou wilt say then unto me, Why doeth he yet find fault? For who hath resisted his will? (20) Nay but, O man, who art thou that repliest against God? Shall the thing formed say to him that formed it, Why hast thou made me thus? (21) Hath not the potter power over the clay, of the same lump to make one vessel unto honour, and another unto dishonour? (22) What if God, willing to shew his wrath, and to make his power known, endured with much longsuffering the vessels of wrath fitted to destruction: (23) And that he might make known the riches of his glory on the vessels of mercy, which he had afore prepared unto glory."*

I've said all this to show that through the untruths [lies, and hypocrisies] of others, misconceptions of God has been fostered, and the fear of God has been cast out. The new idea in Christendom is, God loves everyone, and Jesus died for everyone therefore everyone is heaven bound. Nothing is further from the truth. It's only after they leave this earth and find themselves in torment that they find the truth.

They are relying on the flesh to dictate what truth is, but the flesh never has been a criterion for truth. So many times we fail to understand scriptural truth because we let the flesh get in the way, and believe the flesh over God's word.

Some will say, I don't like it so I won't accept it. If you don't love God's word, it's because you don't love God.

CHAPTER 16

Identifying Mystery Babylon and her Harlot Daughters

First, I implore you to receive my apologies, for I am about to embark on a subject I feel so inadequate to handle. The importance of these truths is of such magnitude that human error and unintentional mistakes can only hinder the facts. Yet the truths which I will seek to uncover have such a need to be revealed and made known, and the burden on my heart is so great that I must do all that I'm able to do. Therefore I ask for you to overlook my bad grammar, poor punctuation, miss spelled words, and poor choices of expressions. I will do my best to express truths in a plain yet concise manor so God will use this to reveal to His elect from within the Babylonian church of their need to escape her grasp and to avoid her plagues.

My information will be of two different sources. First and most important will be the Holy Scriptures, and secondly from recorded history. I will gleam much history from the book "The Two Babylons" authored by Alexander Hislop. First published as a pamphlet in 1853 then printed in book form in 1916. The first American edition was printed in 1943

It is my most earnest prayer that God will use this writing to inform His elect that have been in trapped from within her and misled over the years to see and understand her true identity as well as her harlot daughters and flee from them.

II Corinthians 6:17-18, *"Wherefore come out from among them, and be ye separate, saith the Lord, and touch not the unclean thing; and I will receive you. 18, And will be a Father unto you, and ye shall be my sons and daughters, saith the Lord Almighty."*

During the dark ages little or no records were kept as the saints of God had to go into hiding because of the persecution and slaughter at the hands of the second Babylon. Over fifty million saints were killed in the most horrific ways possible. History teaches us the Church of Rome tried to stamp out of existence the Church that Jesus built. The Dark Ages lasted some twelve hundred years, and were some of the most gruesome years in Church history. The heavy hand of the Catholic Church fell upon the Paulicians, the Arnoldists, The Henricians, Petobrussians, Albigenses, Waldenses, and Ana-Baptist and many others. Many congregations' were completely wiped out of existence. Consequently the Church Jesus built left us with little history during these years. However we are not left in the dark. It seems the Roman church was proud of their murderous activities and kept their own records. Their own words will condemn themselves. The Church that Jesus built was later called the Ana-Baptist, named by the Catholics, and was numerous in number over the land before the Dark Ages began, but after twelve hundred years of persecution their number dwindled to very few. The Church of Rome tried as they could to destroy them from the earth. The persecuting church failed because of Christ's promise to His Church recorded in Matthew 16:18.

Matthew 16:18, *"And I say also unto thee, That thou art Peter, and upon this rock I WILL BUILD MY CHURCH; AND THE GATES OF HELL [Hades] SHALL NOT PREVAIL AGAINST IT."* [Emphases mine.]

Jesus promised His church a perpetual existence from the time he built her during His visit on earth to the time of His return to rapture her back to Himself at the first resurrection. Try as she may, the second Babylonian church could not destroy her. The church Jesus built is recorded in a trail of blood through twelve hundred years of bloodshed but is still here doing what Christ commissioned her to do. God hasn't forgotten her. Notice what John the revelator says about this second Babylon.

Revelation17:6, *"And I saw the woman drunken with the blood of the saints, and the blood of martyrs of Jesus:"*

Revelation 18:24, *"And in her was found the blood of prophets, and of saints, and of all that were slain upon the earth."*

There is coming a day of reconciliation, and double payment will be required of her.

Revelation 18:5-6, *"For her sins have reached unto heaven, and God hath remembered her iniquities. 6. Reward her even as she rewarded you, and double unto her double according to her works: in the cup which she hath filled fill to her double"*

We might say she has more to fear than mere explanations.

The First Babylon

Babylon had Nimrod as its founder. Nimrod was a descendent of Ham. Ham was the youngest of the three sons of Noah It was Ham that displayed immoral acts upon Noah when Noah was drunk with wine.(Genesis 9:21-27) God put a curse upon Ham and his descendants that they would be servants of both Shem and Japeth from that time forward.

Nimrod was a mighty hunter, and went to dwell in the land of Shinar, presently, modern Iraq. Nimrod and his wife Ishtar had a son named Tammuz. Tammuz died as a young adult. Together with his wife, and son they built a city to rival all cities. The hanging gardens of Babylon are one of the seven ancient wonders of the world. Babylon surpasses the grandeur of New York City and the corruption of Chicago.

Nimrod, Isthar, and Tammuz were worshipped as gods, and immortalized as such. A false religion sprang up under the direction of Nimrod and Ishtar. A religion filled with idolatry, and evil traditions that still exists today, and are found within the second Babylon, the Roman Catholic Church.

Their doctrines, practices, and traditions angered God to the point that He confounded their language and spread them around the world. Just as we would do today, the descendants of Babylon took with them their long held traditions. Traditions which God will one day destroy along with the heathens that practice them. This is mystery Babylon, and the mother of harlots. All the traditions from Babylon are alive and well within the Roman Catholic Church.

Revelation 17:1-18 & 18:1-24, *"And there came one of the seven angels which had the seven vials, and talked with me, saying unto me, Come hither; I will show unto thee the judgment of the great whore that sitteth upon many waters: 2. With whom the kings of the earth have committed fornication, and the inhabitants of the earth have been made drunk with the wine of her fornication. 3. So he carried me away in the spirit into the wilderness: and I saw a woman sit upon a scarlet coloured beast, full of names of blasphemy, having seven heads and ten horns. 4. And the woman was arrayed in purple and scarlet colour, and decked with gold and precious stones and pearls, having a golden cup in her hand full of abominations and filthiness of her fornication: 5. And upon her forehead was a name written, MYSTERY BABYLON THE GREAT, THE MOTHER OF HARLOTS AND ABONIMATIONS OF THE EARTH. 6. And I saw the woman drunken with the blood of the saints, and with the blood of the martyrs of Jesus: and when I saw her, I wondered with great admiration. 7. And the angel said unto me, Wherefore didst thou marvel? I will tell thee the mystery of the woman, and the beast that carrieth her, which hath the seven heads and ten horns. 8. The beast that thou sawest was, and is not; and shall ascend out of the bottomless pit, and go into perdition: and they that dwell on the earth shall wonder, whose names were not written in the book of life from before the foundation of the world, when they behold the beast that was, and is not, and yet is. 9. And here is the mind which hath wisdom. The seven heads are seven mountains, on which the woman sitteth. 10. And there are seven kings: five are fallen, and one is, and the other is not yet come; and when he cometh, he must continue a short space. 11. And the beast that was, and is not, even he is the eighth, and is of the seven, and goeth into perdition. 12. And the ten horns which thou sawest are ten kings, which have received no kingdom as yet; but receive power as kings one hour with the beast. 13. These have one mind, and shall give their power and strength unto the beast. 14. These shall make war with the Lamb, and the Lamb shall overcome them: for He is Lord of lords, and*

King of kings: and they that are with him are called and chosen, and faithful. 15. And he saith unto me, The waters which thou sawest, where the whore sitteth, are peoples, and multitudes, and nations, and tongues. 16. And the ten horns which thou sawest upon the beast, these shall hate the whore, and shall make her desolate and naked, and shall eat her flesh, and burn her with fire. 17. For God hath put in their hearts to fulfill his will, and to agree, and give their kingdom unto the beast, until the words of God shall be fulfilled. 18. And the woman which thou sawest is that great city, which reigneth over the kings of the earth."

18:1-24 "And after these things I saw another angel come down from heaven, having great power; and the earth was lightened with his glory. 2. And he cried mightily with a strong voice, saying, Babylon the great is fallen, is fallen, and is become the habitation of devils, and the hold of every foul spirit, and a cage of every unclean and hateful bird. 3. For all nations have drunk of the wine of the wrath of her fornication, and the kings of the earth have committed fornication with her, and the merchants of the earth are waxed rich through the abundance of her delicacies. 4. And I heard another voice from heaven, saying, Come out of her, my people, that ye be not partakers of her sins, and that ye receive not of her plagues. 5. For her sins have reached unto heaven, and God hath remembered her iniquities. 6. Reward her even as she rewarded you, and double unto her double according to her works: in the cup which she hath filled fill to her double. 7. How much she hath glorified herself, and lived deliciously, so much torment and sorrow give her: for she saith in her heart, I sit a queen, and am no widow, and shall see no sorrow. 8. Therefore shall her plagues come in one day, death, and mourning, and famine; and she shall be utterly burned with fire: for strong is the Lord God who judgeth her. 9. And the kings of the earth, who have committed fornication and lived deliciously with her, shall bewail her, and lament for her, when they shall see the smoke of her burning, 10. Standing afar off for the fear of her torment, saying, Alas, alas, that great city Babylon, that mighty city! for in one hour is thy judgment come. 11. And the merchants of the earth shall weep and mourn over her; for no man buyeth their merchandise any more: 12. The merchandise of gold, and silver, and precious stones, and of pearls, and fine linen, and purple, and silk, and scarlet, and all thyine wood, and all manner vessels of ivory, and all manner vessels of most precious wood, and of brass, and iron, and marble, 13. And cinnamon, and odours, and ointments, and frankincense, and wine, and oil, and fine flour, and wheat, and beasts, and sheep, and horses, and chariots, and slaves, and souls of men. 14. And the fruits that thy soul lusted after are departed from thee, and all things which were dainty and goodly are departed from thee, and thou shalt find them no more at all. 15. The merchants of these things, which were made rich by her, shall stand afar off for the fear of her torment, weeping and wailing, And saying, Alas, alas, that great city, that was clothed in fine linen, and purple, and scarlet, and decked with gold, and precious stones, and pearls! 17. For in one hour so great riches is come to naught. And every shipmaster, and all the company in ships, and sailors, and as many as trade by sea, stood afar off, 18. And cried when they saw the smoke of her burning, saying, What city is like unto this great city! 19. And they cast dust on their heads, and cried, weeping and wailing, saying, Alas, alas, that great city, wherein were made rich all that had ships in the sea by reason of her costliness! for in one hour is she made desolate. 20. Rejoice over her, thou heaven, and ye holy apostles and prophets; for God hath avenged you on her. 21. And a mighty angel took up a stone like a great millstone, and cast it into the sea, saying, Thus with violence shall that great city Babylon be thrown down, and shall be found no more at all. 22. And the voice of harpers, and musicians, and of pipers, and trumpeters, shall be heard no more at all in thee; and no craftsman, of whatsoever craft he be, shall be found any more in thee; and the sound of a millstone shall be heard no more at all in thee; 23. And the light of a candle shall shine no more at all in thee; and the voice of the bridegroom and of the bride shall be heard no more at all in thee: for thy merchants were the great men of the earth; for by thy sorceries were all nations deceived. 24. And in her was found the blood of prophets, and of saints, and of all that were slain upon the earth."

There exist two systems of religious thought and tradition that are so much akin to each other that little research needs to be conducted to the understanding of their relationship. Babylon of old and the Roman Catholic Church have the same markings and identifications to each other which bind them together. Just as God once judged Babylon for her sin, God will also judge the great mystery Babylon of today.

In the following pages I will list many, but not all, the comparisons between the two Babylons. Then you decide. Remember Satan tried to destroy the Church that Jesus built and failed. Remember also that Satan is relentless. That is he doesn't give up. If he can't destroy her he will counterfeit her. Satan has many evil and deceivable tools in his arsenal that will entrap many unsuspecting souls into his web. Counterfeiting Christ's church is one way of hindering the Lord's work. The Catholic Church is one of many deceptions. All of her harlot protestant churches are also counterfeit churches, and are deceiving the multitudes by the droves. Many cannot fathom the idea that Satan would or could do such a thing. It would be beneath his character and dignity. We know he tried to destroy her, why not counterfeit her? Satan is an old hand at counterfeiting. He counterfeited the Holy Trinity with an unholy trinity including himself, the antichrist and the false prophet, Angels with demons, the prophets of God with the prophets of Satan [Joseph Smith, Mohammed, and Allah; signs of the Messiah, with false signs, [healings, miracles, and resurrections, the millennium Temple with the tribulation temple. The wedding of the Bride has a false covenant with Israel and the seal of God with the mark of the beast etc., etc.

Satan has and uses only the power God allows him to use. It is up to us to discern under the teaching of the Holy Spirit to discern these truths and apply them to our everyday lives.

Satan has not only counterfeited Christ's church, but also many precious doctrines taught in scripture; doctrines like salvation by grace through faith, with works for salvation, scriptural baptism with baptismal regeneration, sacrificing doctrine for traditions, worshipping God in truth and in spirit with rituals and ceremonies, etc. These are but a few of the tools in his arsenal.

Persecution from the Roman Catholic Church

The Roman Catholic Church had its origin in the third century by the not so great, Constantine. Constantine had ambitions of ruling the world. He knew he had to persuade the Christians to follow him or he would lose in his greedy task. He was himself an evil but very clever man. There were still in those days traditions that came from Babylon; traditions such as a spring celebration, worshipping Cupid, a celebration with colored eggs and rabbits, a fall celebration to worship demons and witches, and a winter celebration to celebrate the birth of Tammuz, Nimrod's son. Now these were all evil pagan celebrations but celebrations that were ingrained into their lives, and not easily removed. These celebrations became the solution to Constantine's problem. All he needed to do is to change the names to Christian names and the gullible Christians would follow his lead.

This was also the beginning of the Catholic Church. Catholic means universal; a universal church that would encompass the world into a one world-wide church, all for the purpose of ruling the world. Soon the true saints of God began to see through his vast schemes, and refused his claims.

Soon laws were passed against these churches that would not follow or join his universal church. As time went by more and more laws were passed to regulate and control this worldly church. Infant baptism and baptismal regeneration became a part of this church. Soon persecution began to fall on the Churches that remained true to the Lord and the scriptures. The universal Catholic Church insisted that the children born into the families of true saints were to be baptized and join the Catholic Church at the threat of death. Most of these saints remained true to their Lord at all costs. Sad to say, there were some that yielded at the fear of death. These were noted by the true churches and non-fellowship was declared between them. These were referred to as irregular or peto-baptist churches.

As time continued the persecution became heavier. Entire churches were slaughtered. Parents had to watch their children massacred at the hands of the Catholic Church. Fifty million saints were slaughtered during these twelve hundred years of the Dark Ages. Read again

> Revelation 17:6, *"And I saw the women drunken with the blood of the saints, and with the blood of the martyrs of Jesus; and when I saw her, I wondered with great admiration."*

> Revelation 18:24. *"And in her was found the blood of prophets, and of saints, and of all that were slain upon the earth."*

Three other books that I strongly recommend everyone to read are "Baptist Faith and Martyrs Fire" by W. J. Burgess, Foxes Christian Martyrs of the World, and the Trail of Blood by J. M. Carroll. During the reformation period when the protestant Churches began to spring up, the persecuted churches first had hope of relief, and some possible help. However such was not the case. These protestant churches only added to the problem. These protestant churches all came out of the mother Catholic Church making them the harlot daughters, and co-conspirators in persecuting the Lord's Church. The Catholic and protestant Churches are reeling in their wealth of today, but a time of reckoning is coming.

The Mother and Child Worship

The worship of Mary and a dependent child is an offspring of the Babylonian religion, and is a carry over into the Catholic Church. This is idolatry in every sense of the word. The Catholic Church takes pride in keeping the child as a dependent infant in the manger, or dead on the cross. This is the reason behind the crucifix with Christ still on the cross.

Christmas

Centuries before the Christian era began and before Jesus was born there was a celebration which originated with the birth of a boy child which correlated with our December 25th. This was a twelve day celebration beginning on the eve of his birthday. This child was worshipped as a god from the time of his birth. He also died as an adult and was deified as a god, and was to be reincarnated every year on his birthday.

On the eve of his birthday a Yule log was placed in a room of the house and overnight it would reincarnate into a beautiful tree decked out with silver and gold.

On the day of his birthday a jolly man in red would give out gifts to children of good behavior. There was the singing of hymns and making merry. Wreaths and mistletoes were used in the celebration just as it is four thousand years later.

It was a time and celebration that angered the God of glory, and it was a part of Babylon. How is it that we can take the same celebration, add Christ's name to it and call it Christian. Wouldn't that actually worsen the sin and anger God even more?

Ezekiel 20:39c, *"Pollute ye my Holy name no more with your gifts, and with your idols."*

Jeremiah 10:1-4, *"Hear ye the word which the LORD speaketh unto you, O house of Israel:2. Thus saith the Lord, Learn not the way of the way of the heathen, and be not dismayed at the signs of heaven; for the heathen are dismayed at them. 3, For the customs of the people are vain: for one cutteth a tree out of the forest, the work of the hands of the workman, with the axe. 4. They deck it with silver and with gold; they fasten it with nails and with hammers, that it move not."*

The decorated tree was to be a sign of the reincarnation of Tammuz, Nimrod's dead son. The decorated tree was the act of the heathen which we Christians are not to learn, yet this act is being taught to Christians all around the world through the efforts of the Great Mystery Babylon Church and her Harlot Daughters.

The puritans, early in American history, understood the evils of this pagan holiday and forbid it from happening. It was then illegal to celebrate Christmas in America.

I know that once Christmas has been ingrained into your life it is a very hard thing to get out. When I was a child I was taught it, and at first I taught it to my children. Then God was pleased to show me the truth. I wrestled until surrendering to God's will. Then I was faced with the task of teaching my children. This was not easy. They yet today celebrate it as a Christian holiday. I can do no more for them but to pray for them. Every year for years I would reinvestigate this time of year to make sure I was right. It was a very difficult thing for me to do. Denying them this time of celebration was hurtful for me for I knew it was hurtful for them as well. My love for my God had to surpass my love for my children.

I have sympathy and understanding for those to whom God has not as of yet showed them this truth. I was once in their category. Perhaps God will use this article to show others as He once showed me.

Easter

Easter isn't even a Christian name. It bears its Chaldean name of Astarte as the queen of heaven. The same was found on the Assyrian monuments as Ishtar, and was the Assyrian goddess.

An egg of wondrous size was to have fallen from heaven into the river Euphrates. The fishes of the river were to have rolled it to the shore where a flock of birds landed to hatch it. Out of it came Venus, who was later called the Syrian goddess. Hence the egg became one of the symbols of Astarte, or Ishtar, and later as Easter.

The Roman Church adopted the mystic egg of Astarte and consecrated it as a symbol of Christ's resurrection. They colored the egg to make it more interesting to the younger set. As always the best and most effective way to develop a following is to begin with the minds of the children.

Rabbits were a sign of fertility. Again they were using the desires of the flesh to persuade the heathen to their side.

Valentine and Halloween

Both valentine and Halloween were rescued from the idolatries of Babylon. This alone should cause the earnest child of God to run from it. Also neither has any scriptural warrant. There are no Biblical teachings, or instructions concerning these, and that alone should steer us away.

Lent

Nimrod's son Tammuz was killed as a young man by a wild boar. His mother Ishtar declared him a god that ascended into heaven. Tammuz became the god of those that worshipped Baal. It was the custom of those in the religion to mourn his *death* for forty days each year.

The weeping for Tammuz is referenced in Ezekiel 8:14. The entire chapter of Ezekiel gives the record of Ezekiel's vision of God's anger at all of the different pagan ceremonies done by the Israelites, including the weeping for Tammuz and worship of the sun

Ezekiel 8:14, *"Then he brought me to the door of the gate of the LORD'S house which was toward the north; and, behold, there sat women weeping for Tammuz."*

Easter is clearly tied to the ritual of lent and set by the appearance of the full moon immediately after the spring equinox.

The early Roman Catholic Church tied together these forty days of mourning, fasting, and sacrifices into their theology of penitence. This personal sacrifice for sin is supposedly to show their dedication to the church, and to Christ. This is works for salvation in the first degree. First, the sacrifice of Christ ended all sacrifice. To say your sacrifice was still needed is to say Christ's sacrifice was insufficient and is a grievous sin within itself.

Lent is not found in the Bible, and did not originate until the year 360 A.D. which was the Council of Laodicea. The Council of Nicaea was held 325 A.D., which established the date for Easter.

Good Friday

One does not have to look far to know that Christ was not crucified on our Friday, a little Bible study and plain mathematics are all you need. All we need to do is count to three, and trust God's word. Let Matthew again instruct us

Matthew 12:39-40, *"But He answered and said unto them, An evil and adulterous generation seeketh after a sign; and there shall be no sign be given to it, but the sign of the prophet Jonah:40. For as Jonah was three days and three nights in the whale's belly; so shall the Son of man be three days and three nights in the heart of the earth."*

The Jewish day begins and ends at sundown, and Jesus was resurrected on the first day of the week. That begins on our Saturday evening. Jesus was resurrected on our Saturday evening.

Matthew 28:1-2. *"In the end of the sabbath, as it began to dawn toward the first day of the week, came Mary Magdalene and the other Mary to see the sepulchre. 2. And, behold, there was a great earthquake: for the angel of the Lord descended from heaven, and came and rolled back the stone from the door, and sat upon it."*

It was late in the evening of Saturday, and about to begin the first day of the week. (Sunday) There was an earthquake just as there was when Christ died on the cross. Mary Magdalene and the other Mary came towards morning prior to the sunrise and found the sepulcher empty. Christ had risen at the earthquake on our Saturday evening before.

Christ was then raised on our Saturday evening, and He was in the sepulchre for three days, and three nights or seventy two hours. Simple math takes us back to His death on the cross as on Wednesday. So why then is Friday chosen by the Catholic Church as the day Christ died? Again it goes back to the festivals in Babylon.

If this wasn't enough, let's go to some other doctrines that are directly contrary to scripture. The Church of Rome has always put tradition over the teachings of God's word, and it shows.

Right in the midst of Saint Peters square stands a large obelisk that once adorned the courtyard of Babylon. This obelisk was rescued and transported to Saint Peters square. This may be the crowning link that ties the Catholic Church to Babylon. The first Babylon was destroyed never to be rebuilt, but the second Babylon is alive and well on planet earth. One day soon that will change also. Revelation 17 & 18 makes that very clear. Little doubt can be left concerning the present day Babylonian Church and her past, but especially her future. God will destroy her in one hour and the world will be watching and wailing for her.

> Revelation 18:9-10, *"And the kings of the earth, who have committed fornication and lived deliciously with her, shall bewail her, and lament for her, when they shall see the smoke of her burning, 10. Standing afar off for the fear of her torment, saying, Alas, alas, that great city Babylon, that mighty city for in one hour is thy judgment come."*

All the wealth she has acquired will do her no good, nor comfort her at all. Trinkets of gold, silver, and precious stone will only add to her judgments and torments. These were objects of idolatry. Countless people who purchased these trinkets were adding to her wealth, and will also add to her judgment.

Universal Church

It was obvious that they were over three hundred years too late to claim to be a part of the Church that Jesus built. The church Jesus built was a local and visible gathering of saints that were baptized by immersion in water. The Catholics timing was over three hundred years too late to claim a partnership with the church that Jesus built. A new approach had to be invented to maintain credibility.

A new concept of church was invented to maintain their credibility in the world. A universal idea of a church would sound good and at the same time fool the multitudes. Of course, this would be completely contrary to scripture and totally the opposite type of church that Jesus built, but who would know? Only the saints of Jesus church, but we will shut them up. A new universal Church could be spread around the world and gather together all nations around the world into one body, and at the same time stamp out this other local church. This new idea of church trumps scripture but this is the least of the concerns to the Catholic Church.

It should become obvious to all the saints of God that a church cannot be both a local body and a world-wide body at the same time. This universal body is nothing less than heresy, and should be labeled as such.

Invisible Church

Some fifteen hundred years after Jesus built His Church the reformation period began. These were faced with much of the same problem that the Catholic Church had. They couldn't claim the true local church, nor could they take on the universal church theory. So they invented yet another idea, that of an invisible church idea. The idea is that all Christians around the world would automatically become a member of one invisible body. This theory teaches that all true Christians are automatically citizens of heaven, and as such will be included in the bride ship of Christ after the first resurrection. This makes baptism useless and a waste of time. It makes local church membership and involvement unimportant. It means participating in the Lord's Supper is of no value. Need I say more? This is heresy in a grand scale.

Only in a local body can one do and be all of these things. Only in a local body can one partake of the Lord's Supper, or be baptized, or be a member. Only in a local church can a church practice discipline as the scriptures teach. Only in the local church can the Gospel be preached. Only in the local church can Christ be glorified.

The universal and invisible church ideas are the inventions of mere depraved and unregenerate man, and are contrary to the Holy Scriptures.

I am tempted to go on and reveal other heresies of the second Mystery Babylon Church. However, I sought only to identify the great mystery Babylonian church, and I feel I have accomplished that. Therefore, I will but mention a few of their many false doctrines without comment.

Baptismal regeneration
Infant Baptism
Justification by works
Sacrifice of the mass
Extreme unction
Purgatory and the prayers for the dead
Idol processions
Relic worship
Rosary
Lamps and candle worship
Cross worship ETC, ETC,

It is not my intention to be offensive even though I'm sure I have been. Please look through any offense you may feel, and compare that I've said with scripture.

This writing has but one purpose and that is to speak to the elect of God from within her that they may escape her, and avoid her plagues.

———∿∾◦◦❦◦◦∾∿———

CHAPTER 17
Eschatology (Last Days)

———∿∾◦◦❦◦◦∾∿———

Introduction

It is certain that Christ is coming again,

Acts 1:9-11, *"And when he had spoken these things, while they beheld, he was taken up; and a cloud received him out of their sight. 10. And while they looked steadfastly toward heaven as he went up, behold, two men stood by them in white apparel; 11. Which also said, Ye men of Galilee, why stand ye gazing up into heaven? This same Jesus, which is taken up from you into heaven, shall so come in like manner as ye have seen him go into heaven."*

M any things of this world remain uncertain, but the rapture (a taking away) is absolutely certain.

By "rapture" we mean this is a time when we will meet the Lord in the air and forever be with Him. Two verses are essential in our understanding of this time.

I Corinthians 15:51-52, *"Behold, I show you a mystery; We shall not all sleep, (die) but we shall all be changed, 52. In a moment, in the twinkling of an eye, at the last trump: for the trumpet shall sound, and the dead shall be raised incorruptible, and we shall be changed."* Emphasis mine LD

I Thessalonians 4:13-18, *"But I would not have you to be ignorant, brethren, concerning them which are asleep, (have died) that ye sorrow not, even as others which have no hope. 14. For if we believe that Jesus died and rose again, even so them also which sleep (are died) in Jesus will God bring with him. 15. For this we say unto you by the word of the Lord, that we which are alive and remain unto the coming of the Lord shall not prevent (precede) them which are asleep. (Are dead) 16. For the Lord himself shall descend from heaven with a shout, with the voice of the archangel, and with the trump of God: and the dead in Christ shall rise first: 17. Then we which are alive and remain shall be caught up together with them in the clouds, to meet the Lord in the air: and so shall we ever be with the Lord. 18. Wherefore comfort one another with these words."* (Emphasis mine LD).

Within the rapture there will be the first resurrection where those who have died in Christ will arise and be united with glorified bodies and meet the Lord in the air. Then those who are yet alive and remain will be changed to receive glorified bodies, and will also rise to meet our Lord in the air and so shall we ever be with our Lord.

The question remains when is Christ coming again?

Matthew 24:35-36 says, *"Heaven and earth shall pass away, But my words shall not pass away. 36. But of the day and hour knoweth no man, no, not the angels of heaven, but my Father only."*

To be sure, we know Jesus is coming again, but the day or time of day no man knows. However, this doesn't mean we are completely left in the dark. I Thessalonians 5:1-9 should not be overlooked.

1 Thessalonians 5:1-9, *"But of the times and the seasons, brethren, ye have no need that I write unto you. 2. For yourselves know perfectly that the day of the Lord so cometh as a thief in the night. 3. For when they shall say, Peace and safety; then sudden destruction cometh upon them, as travail upon a woman with child; and they shall not escape. 4. But ye, brethren, are not in darkness, that that day should overtake you as a thief. 5. Ye are all the children of light, and the children of the day: we are not of the night, nor of darkness. 6. Therefore let us not sleep, as do others; but let us watch and be sober. 7. For they that sleep sleep in the night; and they that be drunken are drunken in the night. 8. But let us, who are of the day, be sober, putting on the breastplate of faith and love; and for a helmet, the hope of salvation. 9. For God hath not appointed us to wrath, but to obtain salvation by our Lord Jesus Christ,"*

The "they" of verse three are unbelievers that are in darkness. The "ye brethren" are believers that are not left in darkness as to the season or closeness of his coming. Even though we know not the day or hour we can know of Christ's coming in relation to Daniel's 70th week. Daniel's seventieth week is a period of seven years (a week of years rather than a week of days) which will culminate or bring to an end the age of the Gentiles in which we now live. We can know the approximate time of Christ coming. This can only be taught by scripture.

Following are some different opinions of this time of Daniel's 70th week. This time is commonly referred to as the tribulation period. However, I think this is in error, but for clarity sake I will use this terminology here.

Pre-trib position says the rapture will precede the tribulation (Daniel's 70th week) and that these seven years are God's wrath on earth. Therefore the rapture must occur prior to this seven year start.

Mid-trib position holds to Christ coming is at the mid-point of Daniel's 70th week and God's wrath doesn't begin until the last half of Daniel's 70th week.

Post-trib position claims the rapture won't happen until Daniel's 70th week is completed.

Pre-wrath position maintains the rapture will occur sometime during the last three and one half years of Daniel's 70th week. This is my position, and by scripture I can prove it.

Pre-millennial accepts all of the fore going positions as all occur prior to Christ's millennial rule on earth.

A-millennial denies the existence of a thousand year rule of Christ. These maintain that Christ is already ruling in the hearts of his people, and that the one thousand years are only figurative or symbolic.

Post-millennial believes the spread of the gospel will evangelize the whole world and bring in a time of complete peace and safety and produce universal salvation for everyone.

Much controversy exists over these positions. Some ask what difference it makes what position we take as long as we believe in something. Prophecy seems unimportant to many, yet one-third of all scripture relates to prophecy. Certainly Christ wants us to know what scripture teaches about last day events. Will Christians one day stand and face antichrist? If so, shouldn't we need to know what's ahead in order to be prepared for him? With this in mind, let's take a look at scripture and leave tradition and human emotion alone. Especially in the day we are now living.

Daniel 9:24-27

Read carefully these verses.

Daniel 9:24-27, *"Seventy weeks are determined upon thy people and upon thy holy city, to finish the transgression, and to make an end of sins, and to make reconciliation for iniquity, and to bring in everlasting righteousness, and to seal up the vision and prophecy, and to anoint the most Holy. 25. Know therefore and understand, that from the going forth of the commandment to restore and to build Jerusalem unto the Messiah the Prince shall be seven weeks, and threescore and two weeks: the street shall be built again, and the wall, even in troublous times. 26. And after threescore and two weeks shall Messiah be cut off, but not for himself: and the people of the prince that shall come shall destroy the city and the sanctuary; and the end thereof shall be with a flood, and unto the end of the war desolations are determined. 27. And he shall confirm the covenant with many for one week: and in the midst of the week he shall cause the sacrifice and the oblation to cease, and for the overspreading of abominations he shall make it desolate, even until the consummation, and that determined shall be poured upon the desolate."*

This prophecy of seventy/seven year periods, each seven years is a week of years. Sixty nine of the seventy weeks have already been fulfilled. This time table first began with Nehemiah 2:1-6 in 445 B.C. Four hundred eighty-three years later Christ was (cut off) crucified. At Christ's crucifixion God's prophetic clock stopped with a final seven years yet to be fulfilled. God's clock will begin again when antichrist confirms a seven year covenant with Israel. (Verse 27) In the middle of these seven years he will break the covenant, and enter the temple to stop the daily sacrifice and commit the abomination of desolation. In so doing he will reveal his true identity and intentions of making the Jews bow at his feet and worship him.

II Thessalonians 2:1-4

2 Thessalonians 2:1-4, *"Now we beseech you, brethren, by the coming of our Lord Jesus Christ, and by our gathering together unto him, 2. That ye be not soon shaken in mind, or be troubled, neither by spirit, nor by word, nor by letter as from us, as that the day of Christ is at hand. 3. Let no man deceive you by any means: for that day shall not come, except there come a falling away first, and that man of sin be revealed, the son of perdition; 4. Who opposeth and exalteth himself above all that is called God, or that is worshipped; so that he as God sitteth in the temple of God, showing himself that he is God."*

Paul is assuring the believers that the rapture had not yet occurred. Paul told them that two specific things must happen before our gathering together unto him which is the rapture. First, antichrist must commit the abomination of desolation which Daniel said won't be until the mid-point of Daniel's seventieth week. That's three and one half years after antichrist makes the seven year covenant. Secondly, there must be a great falling away or apostasy. This also is right at the mid-point of Daniel's seventieth week. When antichrist demands all Jews to bow and worship him or be killed. Many unfaithful Jews will submit in fear. This will be the great falling away. However, many faithful Jews will flee into the wilderness rather then submit to antichrist. To these faithful Jews God will protect and give refuge. Revelation 12:6

Clearly the rapture cannot occur until AFTER the middle of Daniel's seventieth week. Remember God's prophetic clock will begin again at the signing of a covenant between antichrist and the Jews. The rapture will not happen then until sometime AFTER the mid-point of Daniel's 70th week. Thus no one could pin-point the exact day or the time of day.

Olivet Discourse
Matthew 24
Mark 13
Luke 21

Christ's disciples ask Christ a twofold question Matthew 24:3 *"Tell us, when shall these things be? And what shall be the sign of thy coming, and of the end of the world."* The end of the world here is literally the end of the Gentile age. Roman 11:25 *"until the fulness of the Gentiles be come in."* Study carefully Jesus' answers to his disciples' then compare his answer to the first six seals of Revelation chapter six. You will see they are parallel events.

Following is a comparison.

(Olivet Discourse)	(First six seals of Rev. 6)
1. False Christ Matthew 24:5	1. White horse and rider with a crown and bow with no arrow. Rev. 6:1-2
2. Wars and rumors of wars Matthew 24:6	2. Red horse and rider, takes peace from the earth. Killing one another. Rev. 6:3-4
3. Famine and Pestilences Matthew 24:7	3. Black horse and rider with a balance to ration out food. Rev. 6:5-6
4. Persecution and death Matthew 24:9	4. Pale horse and rider, death, and hell follows killing any who would not worship him. Rev. 6:7-8
5. Intensified persecution and killing	5. Souls under the alter who have been killed by antichrist seeking revenge and worship. Rev. 6:9-11

(Note the fifth seal is only a heavenly scene which could not be seen on earth. Therefore, Jesus did not mention this to his disciples in the Olivet Discourse).

6. Strange happenings with the sun, moon, and stars. This I refer to as cosmic disturbances. Matthew 24:29

6. Sun, moon, and stars fall, turn colors, etc. (cosmic disturbances) Rev. 6:12-14

Matthew 24:30 *"And then shall appear the sign of the Son of man in heaven: and then shall all the tribes of the earth mourn, and they shall see the Son of man coming in the clouds of heaven with power and great glory."*

Mark 13:26-27 *"And then shall they see the Son of man coming in the clouds with great power and glory. And then shall he send his angels, and shall gather together his elect from the four winds, from the uttermost part of the earth to the uttermost part of heaven."*

Luke 21:27-28 *"And then shall they see the Son of man coming in a cloud with power and great glory. 28. And when these things begin to pass, then look up, and lift up your heads; for your redemption draweth nigh."*

Revelation 6
1ˢᵗ Six Seals

The first four seals or the four horses of Apocalypse take us from the beginning of Daniel's seventieth week to the mid-point or three and one half years. At the mid-point antichrist commits abomination of desolation by desecrating the temple and declaring himself as ruler and dictator. Demanding all Jews to fall and worship him or be killed. Remember Daniel 9:27 says this will be in the midst of the week.

The fourth seal also begins what Matthew terms as a time of GREAT TRIBULATION such as the world has never seen. Matthew 24:21-22, Mark 13:19-20 God doesn't allow this to continue through to the end of Daniel's seventieth week because it would then destroy his people. God promises protection to his people who remain faithful Matthew 24:13 says, "But he that shall endure unto the end, the same shall be saved," (Delivered) Luke 21:18-19 says, *"But there shall not an hair of your head perish. (19) In your patience possess ye your souls."*

As mentioned previously, Christ gives a list of events that must occur prior to his coming in the clouds for his people, thus destroying the false idea of the imminent return of Christ. The imminent return of Christ suggests two things. **1.** Christ can come at any moment and **2.** No other scripture needs to be yet fulfilled before Christ comes. Both of these ideas are without scriptural warrant.

- II Thessalonians 2:1-4 *Paul clearly teaches that Christ cannot come until the man of sin (antichrist) is revealed.* Daniel 9:27 *says this will not happen until <u>AFTER</u> the mid-point of Daniel's 70ᵗʰ week.*
- The Olivet Discourse must be fulfilled including Revelation 6 from false Christ (1ˢᵗ seal) through to the cosmic disturbances (6ᵗʰ seal).

Revelation 6, 7, and 8

Revelation 6 gives us the first six seals that must be fulfilled before the rapture and as of yet have not been fulfilled. Revelation 7:9-17 Reveals a number of saints too numerous to count. Where did these come from Jesus asked John. John didn't know. Jesus said these are they that just come through the great tribulation. Rev. 7:14 Notice also how they were clothed. Rev. 7:9 They had white robes and palms in their hands. Obviously they had bodies for their white robes, and with hands to hold their palms. The only time saints in glory will receive bodies is at the first resurrection which is also the rapture. Chapter six gives us the six seals before the rapture. Chapter seven gives us the results of the rapture and Chapter eight is the seventh and final seal. The seventh seal initiates God's wrath on a sin ridden, Christ hating world.

Conclusion

Christians will at the end of this Gentile age face a time of testing. All of God's people will one day enjoy God's heavenly Kingdom. However, only those who endure to the end with unwavering devotion will experience the rapture. Those who are truly saved but yet faultier under the testing of antichrist will be killed and go to glory but will miss out on the rapture experience. May God grant me the grace to bare-up under antichrist and so completely trust Him that I may experience the greatest joy ever put upon man?

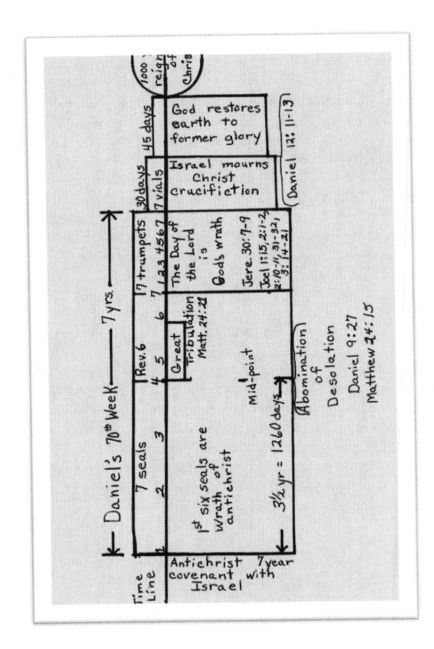

After all human emotion, prejudice, likes and dislikes have been removed it will become very evident that the rapture will occur immediately after the sixth seal and prior to the seventh seal.

The seventh seal initiates the seven trumpets and God's wrath. The seventh trumpet initiates the seven vials. The seven trumpets also is God dealing with the nation of Israel. The seventh trumpet ends the 70ᵗʰ week of Daniel. The seven vials follow Daniel's 70ᵗʰ week and is God's full wrath on all unbelieving Gentiles. This time is also when Israel mourns for having crucified their Messiah. This mourning will last for thirty days. The final forty-five days is Christ restoring the earth back to her former glory right before Christ initiates his millennial reign.

God's Wrath

Acts 2:20 *"The sun shall be turned into darkness, and the moon into blood, <u>before that great and notable day of the Lord come</u>:"* This is the sixth seal happening before God's wrath coming

I Thessalonians 5:9 *"For God hath not appointed us to wrath, but to obtain salvation by our Lord Jesus Christ,"* Believers will never experience God's wrath. Therefore God will remove all believers through rapture prior to His wrath coming down on earth.